Please Don't Tell

Other books by Emma J. Justes

Hearing Beyond the Words

Please Don't Tell

What to Do with the Secrets People Share

Emma J. Justes

Abingdon Press

Nashville

PLEASE DON'T TELL
WHAT TO DO WITH THE SECRETS PEOPLE SHARE

Library of Congress Cataloging-in-Publication Data

Justes, Emma J., 1941-
    Please don't tell : what to do with the secrets people share / Emma J. Justes.
        pages   cm
    Includes bibliographical references.
    ISBN 978-1-4267-7201-6 (alk. paper)
1. Pastoral counseling.   2. Listening—Religious aspects—Christianity.   3. Self-disclosure—Religious aspects—Christianity.   4. Secrecy—Psychological aspects.   5. Trust—Religious aspects—Christianity.
6. Confession.   I. Title.
    BV4012.2.J87 2014
    259—dc23
                                                                        2013035887

Scripture quotations unless noted otherwise are from the Common English Bible. Copyright © 2011 by the Common English Bible. All rights reserved. Used by permission. www.CommonEnglishBible.com.

Scripture quotations marked (NRSV) are taken from New Revised Standard Version of the Bible, copyright 1989, Division of Christian Education of the National Council of the Churches of Christ in the United States of America. Used by permission. All rights reserved.

Disclaimer: All names and significant details have been changed by the author to protect the identity of clients.

14 15 16 17 18 19 20 21 22 23—10 9 8 7 6 5 4 3 2 1
MANUFACTURED IN THE UNITED STATES OF AMERICA

To the memory of my mother, Hazel Katherine Justes

Contents

Acknowledgments

The origins of this project go back to my first years of teaching and the student who returned from an internship to say that she had not been taught anything about ministry with older people during her seminary education. She pushed me into a new area of study and teaching. As a result, I began to listen more carefully to nursing home chaplains, pastors, and to "seasoned saints" themselves. The result was that I began to hear a lot about secrets. This was not a discovery I had anticipated. Over the years of my teaching, the secrets have accumulated from older adults and students as well as from colleagues in teaching and in ministry, and then from my mother. It did not take very long to recognize the importance of having ministers able to hear and accept sometimes painful and always shameful secrets from people of all ages. This work is clearly indebted to that student's shared awareness. Thank you, Gail.

My colleagues in every field at United Theological Seminary have enthusiastically encouraged and supported this work. They have willingly responded to concerns and have offered helpful perspectives. I am indebted to staff members who have been supportive and encouraging, in particular Ramona Jackson, Bridget Weatherspoon, Jim Cottrell, Brice Thomas, Rychie Breidenstein, Caryn Dalton, and Sarah Blair, who graciously stepped up when I needed help. In addition, colleagues Jerome Stevenson, Gary Eubank, and Tom Dozeman have been consistently supportive and encouraging. United provided the sabbatical that made the completion of this work possible, and I am exceedingly thankful.

Two of my dear friends have faithfully read and reread chapter after chapter. The Reverend Jeanette Repp, an Episcopal Priest, persistently offered clarity to the text. Jacqueline Grossmann challenged over and over again what I had thought to be finished and meaningful, leading me to do better work every time. Without their input, this finished product would be greatly diminished. Other friends offered help in research and reading first drafts. Darlene Banks Abernathy became an expert in finding secret stories on the Internet. Amanda Gamboni read some very early work, adding her artistic touch to the help she gave. Sharon Kunselman contributed by reading a draft of the manuscript and with very helpful research. Marge Pauszek gave helpful responses to some of the manuscript and lots of encouragement for the whole project.

In various ways the following faithful people contributed to this word coming into being: Tom Thompson, Brian White, Carla White, Ann Osborn, Beth Anne Crego, William Randolph, Carol Bales, and Cory Rowe.

Friends Julie Hostetter and Kathy Farmer offered consistently enthusiastic support. Marti Anderson graciously gave me support for this project during her lifetime.

I am also indebted to all the people who told me their secrets with the slightest invitation. Whenever and wherever I mentioned that I was writing about secrets, people told me their secrets. This offered more encouragement than I suspect any of you knew, so thank you for that.

Finally, Thelonious Monk, Ray Bailey, and Russell Malone have graciously accompanied me throughout this writing journey with music that sustained my thinking and supported the difficult pauses. I am so appreciative.

Introduction

Whatever is mentionable is
much more manageable.
–Fred Rogers

Dirty little secrets—their reality and power intrude into all our lives, especially if you are in a helping profession, even my own. One nursing home resident, now happily married after two previous divorces, offered this advice, "Tell everyone; it is never too late." She was referring to having told her secret, which she now realized had made her previous marriages unsustainable. She spoke in response to those who questioned whether it is healthy to encourage people to "bring up old stuff."

I have heard many stories of secrets preceded by the words, "I thought I would take this to my grave with me." And "I have never told anyone this before." These words signal the necessity for the person hearing these words to *establish a private sacred space*—realizing how important it is to listen at these moments. One of my hopes is that this book will encourage, support, and contribute to the many people who are open to hear what follows those provocative words. Another hope is that people who hold these secrets will move toward the healing and redemption that follow telling.[1]

My introduction to shame-kept secrets came first from older people and those laypeople, ministers, and chaplains who worked with them. It is important to note that shameful secrets are not limited to those who are older, but it is apparent that some secrets are kept until they can no longer be held. As people anticipate the end of life, they often experience needing "to get something off their chests." Secrets they have kept with shame and, in many cases, an entire lifetime cry out for someone to hear them.

Some nursing or retirement home residents have confessed to their chaplain that they had *wanted* to tell someone before the chaplain came along, but they felt their secrets would not be heard and received. They may have even "tested the waters" by beginning a story and then realized the one listening would not hear the depth of their confession. At last, now someone would listen! Chaplains hear many secrets. What signals do those seniors receive from others that warned them *not* to tell? Pastors and chaplains by virtue of profession hear secrets, but so do lay caregivers. All persons in ministry—lay and clergy—need to discover answers to this question because it will help them serve more effectively and more faithfully.

Secrets, Secrets, Everywhere

We find secrets in scripture, entertainment, government, churches, families, and individuals. Some secrets are not problematic and actually may become life enhancing or life saving. Others are kept in hiding by the shame of the secret keeper. These latter shameful secrets are the focus of this book. Many of the secrets people keep are related to sexual issues, like childhood sexual abuse, but large numbers of them involve unexpected issues. We might expect suicide to be among these secrets, but we do not think of things like literacy, imprisonment, disabilities, mental illness, crimes committed, failures in work and relationships, sexual orientation, adoptions, domestic violence, paternity, and racial or religious identity to be secrets we could encounter. In addition, secrets include stories born by veterans of wars who have returned from battle and never said a word about their experiences to any friends or family. To some extent, these issues and many more may be kept hidden, cloaked in varied degrees of shame. When we recognize the number of shameful secrets held by people we know, those with whom we work, and people in our faith communities, we are astonished.

When I became aware of the prevalence of secret keeping, I began to see it everywhere. Certain talk shows focus on secrets family members have kept from one another, saving them to air in front of a big audience. Mysteries, crime shows, and soap operas depend on carefully hidden secrets. Governments conceal information from their own people as well as from other countries. Not all of these examples are shameful secrets, but they illustrate how common secrets are among us.

Frank Warren began collecting postcard secrets as works of art in 2004. His project has expanded to a blog, PostSecret.com, a travelling exhibit of the postcard artwork he has received and five book volumes.[2] "Post Secret" is a phenomenon. Warren received over 150,000 artful postcard secrets, from all over the world, between 2004 and 2009. Some secrets Warren received (anonymously) were inconsequential, but many were heart wrenching. In his introduction to *A Lifetime of Secrets*, Warren tells us:

> When I told my father I was collecting secrets from strangers for an art project, he didn't know what to think. I tried to explain how the thousands of secrets that had been mailed to me were more than mere confessions. They could be beautiful, funny, sorrowful, inspiring.
>
> "But, Frank," he asked, "why are you soliciting secrets from strangers, and why would anyone tell you a real secret?"

Warren's father spent days visiting his son's exhibit of postcard art in Washington, D.C. and hearing people share how "talking about a painful secret had helped heal a lifelong relationship."

On their way to the airport, for his father's return home, his father broke the silence of their drive to ask, "Do you want to hear my secret?" Then he told Warren about a traumatic childhood experience he had had. This conversation changed Warren's understanding of his father and had a significant impact on their relationship.[3]

We see the seriousness of those secrets shared when we read one of the secrets from *PostSecrets: Confessions on Life, Death, and God,* "I am a Southern Baptist Pastor's Wife. No one knows that I do not believe in God."[4] Surely she could not tell *anyone* else! How important was it to her that *someone* would know her secret?

Warren's work gives us evidence that not all secrets are shameful or painful and still find their way to being *anonymously* shared with a stranger. We find it difficult to imagine how many shameful secrets people keep. Perhaps the revelations of adults who as children were abused by priests brought home to more people the reality of how common shameful secrets are and sparked a new awareness of how powerful the shame can be. When we see how prevalent shame-held secrets are, and the pain with which they are held, we recognize the havoc these secrets create in the lives of individuals and families. Even church communities are not immune. Kept secrets can deeply and negatively affect all the people they touch.

Shame-Filled Secrets in Context

Everyone has secrets. Some are as innocent as keeping secret a birthday surprise. Some are damaging, like having committed a crime and not being caught, everything from shoplifting a candy bar as a child, to having committed or witnessing a murder. Issues of who knows and who doesn't know demand our attention. Some secrets have power and some secrets are neutral. Secrets can heal and secrets can hurt. It depends on what kind of secrets they are, whose secrets they are, why they are kept, by whom they are kept, from whom they are kept, and to whom and when they are finally told.

The focus for this book is on a certain kind of secret that I call a *shameful secret,* which is defined as something kept hidden or unexplained, out of public view, and permeated with shame. Some shameful secrets may be kept for long periods of time, perhaps generations. Secret keepers fear exposure, and sometimes the secrets are kept even from the conscious self. There is a common phrase people say when something unsavory is hidden; they call it a "dirty little secret." However, these secrets are hardly ever "little." Instead, shameful secrets are huge! These secrets are filled with so much shame and pain that they can change people and infect even casual relationships forever.

Identity Formation

The shame-filled secret is not the only kind of secret we keep. We begin to discover secret keeping early in childhood, and secrets play an important role in our development and in our lives within the human community. Early in childhood, secrets play a role in our growth toward becoming separate individuals. Very small children often play at telling secrets when they enlist a parent to listen to a whispered "secret" that turns out to be nothing, just jumbled phrases or sounds—mostly hisses or indistinguishable words. Here they begin to practice sharing "secrets," and begin to recognize the interest others have in secrets and the power secrets hold. The telling of these little "secrets" gives the child a moment of privilege with the parent. This moment of intimacy with the parent contributes to a feeling of being "special" in that relationship, and special among other people who are present (and being excluded) when the "secret" is *privately* shared.

In being able to keep secrets from our parents, especially, we experience steps toward our independence from them, and we move toward formation of an individual identity. Paul Tournier goes so far as to say that *not* being able to keep secrets from parents *prevents one from moving into maturity.*[5] Many of our childhood secrets are harmless to ourselves and others.

As children move into teen years, however, the issue of secret keeping turns another corner, for parents, in particular. Parents sense danger in teens' kept secrets, while teens themselves feel strong needs to exercise their rights of privacy and separation from their parents by keeping secrets. Parents and other adults can struggle with the location of privacy boundaries with not-yet-mature children.

Family Secrets

Some secrets are kept in families because some members of the family are not old enough to receive the information. Young children do not need to know about the rent or the mortgage, nor are they capable of understanding issues related to these major expenses. Sometimes family secrets protect family members from information they do not need or that would be burdensome if they knew and could understand them. These kinds of secrets do not wield power over others; rather they may actually function as a way of caring for others. These are usually issues of privacy.

Children learn that there are matters that are not talked about in the family. It may be clear to the children what is not to be spoken, or it may not be at all clear. The secret's information may remain a mystery to the children of the family, even though they know there is "something." Either way, children grow up knowing about family secret keeping. It may be that Daddy drinks a lot or Mommy swears when no one is around. It may be a secret about a cousin or an uncle, about adultery or another scandal in the past or about specific, present behaviors. It may be about a member of the family who is "institutionalized" with a mental or physical condition or in prison, about which the family is ashamed. There is no conversation about this family member or family incident. Instead they hear, "We do not air our dirty laundry in public."

What happens when the child does not know what the secret is? Secrets in families and churches are often obscured in behaviors that we do not understand. Family members who are not told intuitively recognize that they *must not ask for information* about what they experience. Some of these are family secrets and others may be community-kept secrets.

Communities and churches, as well as families, experience tragedies that may be kept as secrets from the youngest among them or from new arrivals. When the entire community is deeply affected by the event, people are sad and or angry. These emotions may cause the children to feel confused, bewildered, guilty, and afraid.

We, especially, do not want the younger children of three or four to hear the story about what has happened, so we try to shield them from whatever we can. But what does happen to these youngest "victims" is that everybody else acts differently. Their siblings are not the same. The people at church may seem unhappy. Their parents are unusually silent and may be clingy or unusually distant. No one tells these younger kids what happened because we want to protect them. But that does not mean that the little ones do not notice the changes. They can't articulate what they experience, but so much has changed and, strangely, they are likely to feel that it must be their fault. They may begin to feel shame.

This kind of experience can happen on a community-wide basis or on a smaller scale within a family or a church. Here is Josie's story. When she was just a baby her mother sent her to be raised by a relative. After several years passed, Josie was returned to her mother with no explanation. Her mother gave her much more attention than she gave her younger children. This was puzzling to Josie during her childhood.

As an adult Josie found out that her mother had given birth to a child who died a short time before Josie was born. Josie was born too soon for her mother to be able to feel she could keep her. She feared getting attached to this new baby. Years later when Josie was returned, her mother expressed her years of guilt through giving Josie excessive attention. This was very confusing to Josie until she finally heard the story.

Of course, little children should not be burdened with knowing details of some things that happen and some are too young to even begin to understand, but they may need to be told *something*. Otherwise the experience shapes itself into a shameful secret—everyone else is keeping a secret, so they have to, too. Such secrets have power. Maybe later on they finally discover the truth when parents decide they are old enough to hear about it. Or maybe they do not get the story until many years have passed. But by then they have had the experience of what it means to keep a shameful secret. How can we respond to this difficult circumstance, making healing possible?

Happy Secrets

But not all secrets are so onerous; some secrets can be fun. Children learn about expectations of keeping secrets concerning birthday presents or surprises for loved ones. Happy secrets are delightful in family events. On a yearly basis my sons used to try to pry out of me what they were going to get for birthday or Christmas gifts (or even what I was going to give their brother—think of the power this possibility held). I resisted, because I was aware that surprises could be great fun. Waiting to learn what a surprise will be is not easy because this waiting requires mature patience, but the waiting is rewarding.

Inconsequential Secrets

We hold some secrets that are neither damaging nor burdensome. These are truly *little* secrets that do not disrupt relationships or disturb lives. They are just some things we keep to ourselves. They are less involved with power than other secrets. They neither hold power over us, nor do they give us power over others. These secrets are what we might consider to be private. Harriet Lerner draws the distinction between secrets and privacy in terms of impact on self and relationships. Secrecy may be distinguished from privacy when, in secrecy, intentional hiding has a negative impact on any relationships involved.[6]

As adults we may have secrets about what we do privately, perhaps we are compulsive about keeping our home in order, or perhaps we have a harmless guilty pleasure, like enjoying ice cream out of the container. The boundary between such secrets, about which we may be somewhat ashamed, and shameful secrets that become burdensome may be blurred. At what point does a concern and *some shame* become a burden of shame that affects our relationships and our self-esteem? There is no one answer for all situations.

Strategic Secrets

Some secrets are strategic, like my parents' not revealing how they *always knew* when I had not washed my hands when I was a child (just looking at them?).

We are aware of political and business cover-ups that involve "strategic" secrets. These secrets inevitably involve power and the shifting of power. They are usually far from being "little secrets," and may impact the lives of millions of people and entire countries. In general, politics involves a lot of secret keeping. Questions regarding political secret keeping need to focus around issues of who benefits from the secrecy.

Secrets in Scripture

Beginning in Genesis, we find Adam and Eve, having eaten the forbidden fruit, hiding from God—trying to keep their disobedience secret (3:8-13). First they hide, and then they try to deceive God. Adam and Eve are ashamed of their failure to be obedient. Adam blames Eve, and Eve blames the serpent. Of course, they do not succeed at hiding. God already knows. This is only the first of scripture's *many* secrets. This book will focus on two secret-keeping passages that demonstrate current realities of secret keeping and may increase our understanding of how secrets function.

Tamar, a daughter of David, is raped by her half-brother, Amnon, and then told to keep quiet about it by her brother, Absalom (2 Samuel 13:1-22). The outcome of her situation is still familiar today. This story is foreshadowed by the earlier secret David keeps about his rape of Bathsheba and arrangement of the murder of her husband, Uriah.

We also look at Joseph's story. Joseph's brothers sell him into slavery. The brothers lie to their father, telling him that Joseph was killed (Genesis 37–45). They keep this secret from their father for many years. In this story we discover an unexpected outcome of a kept secret when Joseph, the object of the secret, is in the position to rescue his family and all the people of Israel.

Keeping Secrets

Keeping secrets requires acts of acquiring, storing, and recalling memories. We need memories to keep our secrets even though memories have their own failings and peculiarities. Shame functions to require the keeping of the secret, and deceit works with shame to enable the keeping. Of all that is involved in keeping secrets, none of it is easy.

The keeping of a shameful secret requires focus, much like the effort to hold a beach ball underwater. Not wanting anyone to see the secret (the beach ball) makes it necessary to work all the time at keeping it hidden. Any lapse in attention and the ball pops to the surface—the secret is exposed. Hiding a secret takes a great deal of emotional energy.

Choosing to Tell

Deciding to tell a shame-filled secret is very difficult. This book offers readers understanding of ways secret keepers think through telling and consider what the outcomes could be. Telling a secret will create change in the teller's life and in the lives of others related to the teller or, related, in other ways, to the secret. Change, as it always does, will mean loss (as well as potential gain) in the secret keeper's life. Awareness of possible losses contributes to the difficulty of deciding to tell. We recognize that telling secrets involves a loss of control—we are in control of the secret's contents until we tell. When secret keepers recognize the presence of the boundless love of God that we find represented by the father in the parable of the prodigal son (Luke 15:11-32), telling becomes possible. Secret keepers see hope as what they can *imagine* on the other side of telling, instead of the loss, judgment, and rejection they have anticipated. While telling still has repercussions, the secret keeper now faces them with hope as well as fear.

Listening to Secrets

Listening to secrets is difficult. Pastors, chaplains, church leaders, and family members are often in situations in which they *could* hear secrets. But sometimes our own secrets, issues, and pains get in the way of our being able to hear the secrets of others. *We are better listeners when we do not feel judgmental or fragile.* In addition, those who listen to confessions of secrets need to be capable of embodying the ability to both receive and to bear heavy secrets. This ability is not demonstrated through arrogance (i.e., an attitude that says, "I'm so tough that I can take anything you tell me"), but by means of strength shown through humility through the ability to listen well and to receive what comes to them and not hide or run from it (i.e., an attitude that says, "I care about you so much that I'm here to walk with you").

Anyone who listens to secrets also needs to be aware that hearing has the possibility of *changing the listener* as well as the speaker. The experience of hearing involves being vulnerable and yet having strong self boundaries. Yet, sometimes our own resistance can cause us to avoid hearing. Here it is also important to note that listening to our own inner voice is important, especially if the prospect of listening makes us unduly anxious or fearful. No one can listen to everyone's secrets. If we find ourselves avoiding, not listening, or even thinking of something else when people are confiding in us, it can be better to guide that person to another caregiver. Part of being an effective and competent caregiver is knowing your limits.

Meeting a Secret

We never know when we will be told a secret. The following story was my initiation into the world of shameful secrets. It was instrumental in my seeking deeper understanding of secrets and their impact on the lives of their keepers. Religious communities are filled with people who carry secrets like this one—secrets that need to be told and heard. The speaker had been a faithful church member for many years when she told her secret.

She began, "I thought I would take this to my grave with me. I've never told anyone this before." These are the words of my mother when she was seventy-six years old. This was how she began to tell me that her father had sexually abused her from the time she was seven years old until she left home in late adolescence. She went on to describe her memories of her father's abuse of her and her suspicions about his abuse of at least some of her five siblings. She expressed feelings of disgust and anger, but not before she paused and asked, "Well, what do you think of your mother now?"

Even though we had a strong relationship, she felt unsure about how I would see her once I knew the truth about her secret. My mother had never had the experience of telling *anyone* her secret. What was she to expect as a response to her telling? She had lived seven decades with the decision that it was too great a risk to find out how someone would react. I recognize now, that from the moment my mother said that she had never told anyone before, I had moved into a *sacred space with her.* I did not name it that at the time and could only do so in retrospect. Now, however, I am aware that this holy space is where every listener stands each time a shameful secret is confessed.

A door was opened for her to tell—prompted by my finally admitting out loud, "I *never* liked your father (note: I didn't call him *my grandfather*)." My response to her telling, rather than changing my view of her, was an experience of life pieces tumbling into place. Suddenly past confusion made sense in our family life and in my own adult life. I had a clear recognition of having somehow "known" what she had just told me.[7] Her telling and my hearing about her horrible experience turned out to be very life affirming for both of us—for me to finally, truly *know,* and for her to finally speak the secret. With the speaking of the secret, shame often begins to fade and affirmation of life begins to emerge.

This encounter was only the beginning of a long series of conversations between us that extended over the final twelve years of her life. Mother had never before told anyone about her life-shaping experience of abuse. Following her telling, every time we were together until shortly before she died, the secret became a part of our conversations. Sometimes she repeated the same things. Other times she added new dimensions of experience or feelings remembered and, now, revealed. Her process was much like the grieving we go through when we experience an important loss. We struggle over time to find the place and meaning in our lives of grief with which we struggle. Our healing takes place in repeating and reviewing—*when* someone hears us.

The depth of her rage about the abuse she experienced from her father was startling for me to see. What she experienced at the hands of her father was a violation of her life as well as her body. What possibilities in her life were never realized because of ways the secret shaped her life? How had feelings toward her father and about herself as a result of the abuse shaped her life? How had her secret shaped her relationships? Expressing her rage for the first time in her life made it more real and at the same time allowed it to diminish. She continued to put the pieces together and move toward healing—making some peace with her past.

Sometime after telling me her secret, mother also told her pastor. They already had a special relationship, and I was very glad she had him to share in her secret as well. I am aware of the complete trust she had in him and the kindness, care, and the absence of judgment that he embodied.

Having grown up in a family in which a secret was kept, I experienced and witnessed the toll secret keeping has on those who carry shameful secrets, and on those who are close to them. I realize how important it is for keepers of shameful secrets to reveal their secrets and be able to heal. Many members of faith communities carry secrets much like my mother's. I know that telling secrets may mean healing for others who have not previously known the secrets—to hear secrets that have shaped their relationships and affected their lives.

Overview

I hope that through this book readers may come to realize that keeping shameful secrets is *not actually a private matter.* Kept secrets affect both small and large communities. We see that some secret keeping—like confidentiality and secrets that protect others in different ways—is positive. At the same time we should realize that *the fabric of the human community is damaged by much of our secret keeping.* Issues of anger and low self-esteem are carried throughout lifetimes, affecting families and communities.

Please Don't Tell: What to Do with Secrets People Share offers preparation for those who are willing to be hearers of secrets. Even though I write from a Protestant Christian perspective, the issues and concerns I am dealing with span faiths and denominations. My faith perspective does not bind my hopes for what this work will accomplish. Chapter 1, *Hearing Confessions: How to Help People Tell You What They Need to Tell*, provides understanding of how to open doors so that secret keepers who need to speak can begin to confess. Facilitating people to tell also relies on the character of the listener—reflected in the communication of hospitality, acceptance, openness, and grace, as well as the willingness to talk about difficult issues.

My mother's secret provides an entrée into looking at some elements of kept secrets. The many functions of secrets in our lives demonstrate that secrets themselves are not the problem, but the *nature of the secrets kept* and the *feelings regarding the secrets kept* create struggles, encourage hiding, shape relationships, and diminish lives. Because so many of us in ministry also carry our own secrets, we must use caution to avoid, as chapter 2 warns, "trading secrets." In general, we do not enable healing when we impose our own secrets (or secrets we have heard) on others, while they are telling their secrets. Our impulse to tell our own stories is rarely, if ever, helpful. This chapter further reminds us that the responsibility of the pastor is not only to hear secrets but also to deal with them with integrity, respect, and discretion, and within denominational and legal boundaries. Listeners, both during and after hearing, must be very clear about the boundaries necessary to hold secrets told.

Persons in ministry may be those most likely to hear painful secrets. Secrets emerge at life-changing moments—a death or approaching death, during serious illness, the birth of a child, or a wedding. Pastors are usually there for those moments and often play roles central in these life-defining times. Although this book is particularly intended for persons in ministry, both clergy and lay ministries, it is not limited to their use. Church members may, through the workshops offered at the end of the book, become involved in learning more about hearing secrets and participating in a healing ministry to those who choose to tell their secrets. Whoever receives secrets realizes that they carry the burden of keeping those secrets. Chapter 3 deals with how one can continue to hear and bear painful secrets as we offer ministry to those who need to tell.

As we continue into the following chapters we engage in discussions of particular elements of keeping secrets. Chapters 4, 5, and 6 present discussions of lying, shame, and memory as they play roles essential to the keeping of secrets. We consider questions about whether what we hear is true; whether shame can allow the release of secrets, and whether reliable memories emerge when shameful secrets are confessed.

We all keep secrets. Churches and families, as well as individuals, keep secrets and pass them on from one generation to another without new members of the church or family actually knowing what the secrets are, but clearly joining in carrying the shared burdens. Chapter 7 opens this discussion with the story of David and Bathsheba and its ongoing impact on David's family and kingdom as we read in 2 Samuel.

I offer a theological framework rooted in the grace of God, as demonstrated in the parable of the Prodigal Son. There we find our foundation for listening to secrets. Chapter 8 presents God's grace that allows for the welcoming of the secret, and the acceptance of the secret keeper. Through offering hospitality, the receiver of the secret embodies God's grace and God's love to the secret keeper. Shame-experiencing secret keepers find support for telling secrets, with the possibility of hope at the other side of the telling. Redemption and renewal become possible, regardless of whether the secret is the experience of an individual, a family, or a community, or whether the impact of the secret has crossed from generation to generation. The grace of God becomes the heart of receiving confessed secrets and the healing of those who have been burdened by the secrets.

The stories of told secrets in this book have been altered or compiled from a mixture of stories. The exception to this is found in direct quotations. No names of actual persons involved are revealed.

Four workshops are offered at the end of the book to help laypeople work on skills and awareness for the purpose of being able to listen to the secrets others need to confess.

Chapter 1

Hearing Confessions

How to Help People Tell You What They Need to Tell

Introduction

The church has a long history of hearing confessions. What many recognize is the image of the Roman Catholic confessional, where parishioners anonymously confess their sins to the priest and receive penance and absolution. Historically, parishioners had to make confession every week in order to be able to participate in the Mass. The confessional is designed for the priest to hear what parishioners identify as sins they have committed (based in the Ten Commandments), for which they need God's forgiveness. The confidentiality of what is confessed to the priest is absolute. The confessional assures confidentiality.

While most Protestant churches do not have this same tradition, receiving confessions has remained an important function in ministry across the church. Pastors do not always welcome confessions. After all, traditionally, the priest hears confessions *without* being face-to-face with a parishioner. Being able to listen to something clergy do not really want to hear can be difficult to "face."

Confidentiality remains an important dimension for all clergy hearing confessions, but most other clergy have not usually had the same legal immunity that the Roman Catholic confessional has held. The understanding of confession in this book differs somewhat from the traditional understanding of confessing sins. We also are concerned about secrets people confess that may not be considered by them to be *their* sins. They sometimes carry and confess shameful secrets about what someone else has done.

This chapter deals with issues of receiving what is confessed and offers help to caregivers who want to be able to hear *whatever* people need to confess. We find ourselves in the position of being able to play a role in helping people finally tell the secrets they want to confess. Our focus here is on secrets people keep, noting that *confessions usually (if not always) involve secrets.*

Many secrets are kept with shame. When the secret is revealed both *the secret and the speaker are exposed.* The confession of a secret occurs when the speaker makes the difficult decision to tell. Secret keepers need a safe "place" that includes someone who will be able to listen and truly hear the depth of the secret and, further, be trusted to respect appropriate boundaries,[1] in hearing and keeping the secret.

Secret keepers realize that not everyone *does* listen. Just because pastors are those who hear confessions, and are people one should be able to trust, does not mean a particular person in ministry can be recognized as one who will be able to listen to a secret. We have ways to communicate that we do not want to hear some of the dreadful stuff people need to tell. All of us need to recognize ways in which we convey that we are closed to hearing what someone needs to tell.

Listening is not easy, even though we often presume that we listen and hear one another. Listening to a secret that is filled with shame demands more effort than most of what we hear from any speaker. Hearing doesn't end with listening, but continues into *responding appropriately* to what has been heard, and beyond response, to the "keeping" of the secret.

Although we may think that we like to hear secrets, in the midst of listening we discover that with their telling come the strong feelings of the speaker—feelings of shame, anger, grief, pain, and low self-esteem. These can be difficult emotions for us to handle. They may be feelings that we prefer to avoid hearing. The strength of their feelings touches our own feelings, and this contributes to making listening difficult. We *can* prepare ourselves to receive confessions of secrets, however, and to respond to them. *After* hearing secrets we also have to *find ways that let the speaker know we have heard the very worst of their confessions.*

Another difficulty in hearing secrets involves our being able to be aware of and keep appropriate boundaries. We must be able to do this both as we listen and after we have heard the confessed secret. We have more difficulty hearing secrets when we are unsure or tentative in our boundary keeping. We need to know our boundaries in relationship with the confessor, trust ourselves to keep them, and not use the knowledge of his or her secret to our own advantage in our relationship with him or her or anywhere else. When we are secure in our boundaries, we provide the feeling of safety that secret telling requires. Boundaries are discussed more fully in chapter 2.

This chapter helps those who want to be able to hear secrets of others become able to do so, and also enables those who listen to assure secret keepers that they can be safe in confessing. Through our character we let others know that we can and will hear them. Restoration begins when secrets are heard, and the keeper of the secret moves toward healing.[2] The grace of God makes renewal available.

Part I: Listening: Not as Easy as It Sounds

Fears Limit What We Hear

Some issues frighten those who try to listen—often because these particular issues touch our own feelings. Listeners need to become aware of what the difficult issues are for them and why they are troublesome. This awareness helps a listener avoid disengaging, judging, or otherwise demonstrating fear. It is not just a matter of what specifically relates to our own experiences, but many of us have trouble listening to broader issues related to sex, violence, conflict, or even death.

One fear is that we will not be adequate listeners. We don't know enough about the issue raised. Also, will we understand what is needed from us? Will we know what to say or do in response to what was said? The responsibility of being a listener to kept secrets feels heavy. It is. It may be important *not* to say or do anything more than listen. Coming to realize *that there is not one correct response* to hearing a secret may ease some of our fears. Hearing the secret and taking the secret teller seriously are the most important things listeners can do. Then we make decisions about what follow-up may be necessary. This could include making a referral.

When a Listener Does Not Want to Hear

When someone begins, "I have never told anyone this before," the listener (who is not sure about hearing something which is secret) may respond (or feel like responding), "Are you certain you want to tell it now? To me?" These questions, when spoken, signal the speaker that you are not certain about hearing the secret—perhaps you feel you are not the right person to listen. Alternatively, it also could be a helpful response, when it calls the person's attention to where they are headed—that they are about to reveal something significant. In asking this or a similar question, the listener invites, and maybe encourages, the teller to reconsider. The problem is that it may also communicate to the speaker to stop. The tone of how the question is asked makes the difference between whether it is encouraging or a signal that says, "Please stop." The tone is informed by the listener's purpose for this caution. Is the listener seeking to protect him- or herself or to protect the speaker? Only the latter is valid.

Experience reveals that once a person has said, "I have never told anyone this before," the person has probably already decided to tell, so any caution to reconsider may be ineffective. As we consider all that may go into deciding to tell, we begin to recognize that once the decision is made, the process has begun.

For the listener who clearly does *not* want to hear or does not feel capable of hearing, this is the time to warn the secret keeper. "I am not sure I am the best person to hear something so important. I will help you find someone who can listen to you." This kind of response can be crushing to someone who has probably taken a long time to decide to tell and carefully chosen the hearer. Stopping a person at this point, however, will not be as bad as allowing the person to confess a shameful secret when we cannot graciously listen and truly hear both the content and the meaning of the secret. The refusal to hear the secret may feel like rejection to the person who wants to tell, but it is better to warn them before they tell than after. After telling, they will have become more vulnerable with the exposure of their secret and its shame. Not being able to receive, honor, and respect what will be said means one should not be the one who hears.

It is so easy to convey to others that we would rather not know. "Too much information!" we signal. Of course, we also may struggle with our own curiosity about what the confessor will say, alongside our fear of hearing. Hearing shameful secrets confessed can be very unpleasant, disturbing, messy stuff. Curiosity will not carry you very far in caring for the secret teller. While it may be enticing, do not listen solely out of curiosity.

We become vulnerable in hearing the difficult emotions of secret keepers. We need to be as "shockproof" as possible, so we can have the courage to listen when we have heard the warning that a secret is coming. In considering an inability to hear someone's secret, the listener should recognize this potential concern: How can a listener's unwillingness or inability to listen to the secret be communicated so that the teller does not feel more shame, after having told? Recognize this as an important question.

Problems in Listening

Even good listeners may stumble when it comes to hearing an unexpected secret that is full of shame. With awareness about the process of arriving at telling a secret, the willing listener can be alert to circumstances that have the potential to release kept secrets.

Preparing oneself to listen to painful secrets does not give anyone a license to push others to reveal secrets. We may have experiences with an individual that caused us to suspect the person was keeping a shameful secret. However, the secret keeper must freely make the choice whether to tell and decide on the timing of telling. We do not have the option to "guess" what secret a person may hold. We do have the opportunity to *prepare the context* for a person to tell their secrets. This is not the same as urging them to tell, seducing, forcing, manipulating, or tricking them into telling. Being alert and open to hearing is very different from urging someone to tell or trying to guess what their secret is.

As a listener who receives a secret, know that the secret will most likely be told again and again. Be ready to hear it again and again, especially when you are the only one who was told. There is much to unpack in shameful secrets. Feelings may become deeper, and details may emerge more clearly, or even change somewhat. The impact of the secret on the keeper's life may be reviewed and reassessed. The secret keeper makes decisions about telling anyone else while considering others who have been involved in the secret's creation or existence.

Hearing oneself speak the secret enables the teller to bring it into reality so it can be placed in the present. The listener may encourage greater or deeper exploration of parts of the secret that may be helpful for the teller. It may become difficult for the listener to hear the secret and its enhancements over time. We may even try to avoid the secret teller, because the secret is so hard (or becomes boring) to hear over and over. Self-awareness is a key, so that we can act appropriately instead of being controlled by our own discomfort or impatience. As we listen, we can challenge ourselves to be attentive for hints of something new, and invite reflection on what we have heard that was different.

The teller and the listener both become vulnerable whenever secrets are told. We do not want to go where *we* will be vulnerable. Listeners are vulnerable because we enter and stand on sacred ground. What we hear may touch painful places in ourselves. We are also vulnerable because we are not able to heal the hurt we hear, we cannot alter the past, we do not have answers, and we are receivers and holders. Experienced pastor and author Ronald Richardson makes this point: "Understanding people is more important than trying to do something to people, to 'fix' them in some way."[3] Being a solver or a fixer always feels less vulnerable, but instead we trust in the healing that the telling itself initiates, through the grace of God.

In light of the presence and availability of God's grace, perhaps we are better able to face our vulnerability. We, too, stand in the grace of God. The listener also becomes vulnerable when the secret we hear challenges the view we have held of the secret teller. Our own abilities to assess who someone is and what they are like may be shattered when we hear their secret. A church leader may suddenly seem like a stranger, but must not be treated and left as a stranger by the skilled listener.

Once a secret is confessed, issues of closeness or distance sometimes emerge. Closeness could result from the level of intimacy shared in the spoken secret. It may mean that the speaker feels much closer to the hearer and may even anticipate reciprocal intimacy from the hearer in terms of expecting the listener to share a secret of his or her own. Alternatively, the listener in hearing the secret may experience more closeness with the speaker than feels comfortable to her or him. Either of these experiences involves vulnerability and requires self-awareness and reliable boundaries.

Part II: Opening Doors for Telling

The Opened Doors

The foundation for any telling is that the secret keeper experiences a trust in the person who is told. When we are trustworthy, we open doors for sharing of deeply hidden pains and struggles. In other ways we signal that we are able to hear about some shameful secrets. Events offer opportunities for telling a secret.

Shirley's Story. A pastor who had served a particular church for several years initiated a series of adult classes dealing with human sexuality. Approximately a dozen adults attended the series. Their ages ranged from early twenties into the seventies. Discussion was open and lively. Following the three-week series, while people were still leaving the fellowship hall, a woman whom I will call Shirley spoke to the pastor. At the time of this class, Shirley was over seventy years old.

Shirley began with the familiar introduction to a long-kept secret, "I have never told anyone this before." Whenever this phrase is used, it is clear that shame is right ahead and clearly involved in what is going to be said. Shirley told about when she was a young girl. Some older boys from her neighborhood had gotten her alone and fondled her. She was neither raped nor physically hurt, but the terror and shame of the experience never left her.

She was devastated from the event itself and as a result of its aftermath. She remembered how the same boys laughed at her whenever they saw her at school and in town, and how embarrassed she was every time. The town was too small to be able to avoid them. Their continued reminders of the experience reinforced her shame. Not only was she assaulted; she was betrayed and repeatedly belittled by her tormentors. This experience stayed with Shirley for the rest of her life.

Shirley told her pastor that after that experience she "never could trust men." She reflected that this experience was probably why she never married. Shirley was aware of some of the ways her experience (which some would see as harmless) had defined her life. I wonder if there was more pain in her life that she could have connected to the experience. I wonder how the keeping of the secret itself added to the burden of the event. Her shameful experience diminished her ability to relate to men, profoundly impacting her life.

Why Didn't Shirley Tell? Why didn't Shirley, as a young girl, tell anyone about what had happened? She was apparently immediately ashamed of what had happened to her. Clearly the boys were in the wrong. She was young and may have, at the beginning, enjoyed the attention of older boys. She told her pastor that she had "developed early," which might have contributed to the boys making her a target for their assault. This was what she supposed.

Young girls who develop early sometimes experience shame about their bodies, even without the negative attention it may attract. At the time when she was growing up, little, if anything, was said about sex, so adolescence was a painful mystery for many young girls, especially when their sexuality became obvious before others of their age. Shame was upon Shirley even before the boys were. Without being able to tell anyone about her experience and with the continued taunting of the boys, Shirley was left with her secret and with her hurt, anger, frustration, and diminished self-esteem. She could not do anything to protect herself from the embarrassment heaped upon her. Her reaction was to become certain that males could not be trusted.

Besides her mistrust of men, perhaps the keeping of this shameful secret *distracted* Shirley from focusing on, from giving full attention to, other things in her life—from the use of her gifts. Shirley, as the pastor knew her, was active in the church, attending regularly. She came for special events, but she never took a leadership role. She had obtained only a high school education, like many women of her era. Shirley had worked and lived her life under a secret cloud of shame.

Who Could She Have Told? In the 1930s, when Shirley was a young girl, sex was not discussed. Abuse was not commonly acknowledged. I don't know about her family, but clearly she didn't feel there was anyone she could have told—not even a girlfriend. She would have been too ashamed to tell anyone. Shirley might have anticipated being judged by others for having been with the boys, having "let them do it." Had she told, she might have been disparaged for making too much out of such an insignificant event. Where was a safe place in her life where she would be free to tell her secret? Where would she not be laughed at, judged, or condemned? Shirley didn't find this place until she was past seventy years old. Then she found it with her pastor.

Why Now? In the context of the adult class at church that focused on human sexuality, her pastor, who was a woman, raised issues of sexual abuse. The mention of sexual abuse and the trust relationship she had with her pastor—probably including the fact that her pastor was a woman—combined to make it possible for her to speak a secret of more than sixty years.

I do not know if Shirley had ever had a female pastor before or how much she had been able to trust the men who had been her pastors. Had she been able to entrust men with her spiritual life in light of her secret and her mistrust of men? From what Shirley said about her story, her mistrust did not distinguish between every man and every clergyman.

This first telling of her story was only the beginning of what needed to happen for Shirley to heal the wounds of her secret. Her telling was received with understanding, so she was able to continue toward healing. If her experience had been viewed as unimportant and taken lightly by her pastor, it would have meant that Shirley's experience would return to secret status and any further processing would have been put to rest.

Saying to Shirley, "They didn't *really* hurt you, did they?" or "How could that have been something so important to remember this long?" These responses would mean that Shirley's experience was discounted, even though it might have made the listener more comfortable. Questions could be asked to clarify or invite her to further describe her experience, but any hint at accusing, diminishing, judging, or doubting her experience had to be avoided.

We see in Shirley's story one example of how a door can be opened for the telling of a secret. When Shirley participated in a class that openly faced the issue of sexual abuse, she felt freed to confess a long-term secret. When I told my mother that I never liked her father, she was freed to tell me about his abuse. We can find many ways to create openings or open doors for people to tell secrets.

Another Door Opened

A pastor told me about his experience: "Dan" was the pastor of a medium-sized church of a mainline denomination. He had been in ministry a dozen years and at this church for the past three years. He had become acquainted with the people of the church and the community and felt he knew them fairly well.

When National Domestic Violence Awareness Week came around, he made a courageous decision to deal with domestic violence in his sermon. He prepared a recording of a single chime being played every fifteen seconds.[4] As he preached, the recording played. At first it was apparent that people in the congregation were disturbed by the repeating sound, but after a while, the people did not seem to notice it any more.

Finally, in the sermon, he mentioned that it was the beginning of Domestic Violence Awareness Week, quoted statistics about how often domestic abuse occurs, and told the congregation that the chimes had represented each woman abused during the length of the sermon. He commented that the congregation's ability to tune out the sound of the chimes was much like the church tuning out on the issue of domestic violence and failing to take responsibility in addressing the issue. He shared, "In the closing prayer I asked God's protection for families facing violence, forgiveness for the church's silence, and courage to make a change in the situation."

In the days following the sermon, five women spoke to him about having been victims of violence in their own homes. He was not aware of the experiences of these women prior to that Sunday. They had kept secret their experiences with domestic violence until they realized there was someone who could hear. This experience was similar to Shirley's. Shirley heard someone willing to speak about domestic violence and this opened the door for her to tell her sixty-year-old secret.

The first woman to approach Dan after the service was in her seventies and reported she had been living separated from her abusive husband for twenty-eight years. The church assumed that she was a widow, and she wanted to keep it that way. Pastor Dan promised her that her secret was safe with him and he assured her that there was no need for her to feel guilt or shame. Some time following this conversation her pastor reported a change in their relationship, "There seems to be a closer bond with her."

Four more women spoke to the pastor. One thing that emerged from what the pastor reported, was a concern on the part of women that they would be judged by the church, if others knew what they experienced, or if they got a divorce. Some of the women reported situations that included violence toward the children in their family, alcoholism, and sexual violation. There they were stuck with abuse and with keeping it secret, clearly fearing the judgment of the church.

From this experience in a single church and the statistics on domestic violence, we might expect many more secrets within congregations regarding domestic violence. Pastor Dan had signaled his awareness of domestic violence and opened the door for the women to speak. All of the women started out by saying, "I have never told this to anyone" or "Only my children know." Assurance of how Pastor Dan now felt about them was in their hearts even before he responded to what they told him.

Other Openings

Doors can be opened in another way when we are able to invite people to talk about their life experiences or give people opportunities to explore their lives by engaging them in what is called "life-review."[5] Questions that ask, "What has been your greatest accomplishment in life so far?" or "What is your greatest disappointment?" or "What do you regret?"[6] may be helpful in opening doors. These questions for life review may be more appropriate for older persons. When the listener has proven to be a trustworthy person, the speaker may come up with surprising secrets. For this to happen requires that the person initiating the question will *wait, silently,* patiently, for an answer.

Hints That May Be Clues about Secrets

When we are given a hint that seems to point to a deeper issue—perhaps a secret—we can follow that hint with expression of concern about what was heard. "I am curious about what you meant when you referred to your wedding. I heard an interesting tone in your voice." We can communicate in many ways that we heard something about which we are curious. Sometimes we are immediately aware of this "clue" moment. Other times it may dawn on us later, but it is not too late to initiate another conversation and call the clue to the speaker's attention, "I heard something I wondered about. We didn't get to talk about it. Maybe we can do so later." These reflections do not have to come in the form of questions.

We can pave the way for secret tellers by demonstrating that we can speak about difficult issues like death, sex, violence, and abuse. We can signal our willingness and ability to hear and respond. We can provide settings for confessing and avenues for realizing what has been hidden. The person must determine whether to tell without persuasion, manipulation, or probing. *They* get to choose to keep or to expose their secret.

Part III: The Power of Listening

Hearing as Healing

When we express a clear awareness of the boundless love of God available for ourselves and others, we are able to be a bridge for others to be able to come to this reality themselves. Secret keepers are enabled to break their silence when they no longer anticipate judgment. Ministry is not entirely in what we do, but more important, it lies in the character of who we are—our being—as well as in our doing. Our own awareness and embodiment of God's boundless love deeply affect our way of being. As we embody God's love and grace, we open doors for people to confess shameful secrets.

The importance of being heard and what it means to the one who is heard varies with the importance of the message. When we realize that the speaker is confessing a painful secret that was, in some cases, hidden over many years' time and carried painful feelings of shame, anger, loss, and fear, we must realize that the importance of being heard is at its highest level.

After telling, healing can continue internally, as secret tellers continue to put pieces together and move beyond their hiding. Healing also may rely on having someone to talk with about the secret over a period of time. Healing may include forgiveness of one's self or of others. Listeners should not make it *their* priority that the secret keeper forgives someone who has caused them pain. Forgiveness may be part of the conversations but not made a pressured priority. Forgiving is up to the secret keeper—resting entirely on their ability to forgive and readiness to do so. The hearer may help him or her come to deeper understandings of forgiveness and the importance of forgiving themselves when the secret keeper expresses this need. Demanding that secret keepers forgive when they are not able to is a route toward increased shame. Now they can add this failure to their shame.

The Role of Awareness in Preparing to Listen

We often function in our lives and in ministry without the full awareness we need to be able to recognize what is going on in the lives of the people to whom we offer ministry. At the same time, we fail to function with a full self-awareness that provides a presence that enriches our ministry.

Attentiveness to the presence of the grace of God is of primary importance as we prepare to listen. I think of the grace of God as *always* available to us—*all of us*. When we can be open to what God's grace brings to us in any moment, we enter into care for others with benefits beyond our understanding. When we plunge ahead oblivious to, or in denial of, the accessibility of God's grace through the Holy Spirit, we may not bring into the sacred space of confession the fullness of God's healing gifts that can come through us. However, we are still able to move ahead in listening and care without this awareness and then discover, in the process, how grace breaks in upon us. At that point, we rely on our being able to receive what God's grace brings to us, for that moment, and allow it to make use of us in a way that is transformative for us as well as for a speaker. Of course, allowing God's grace to break in on what we do means we have to be vulnerable and not in control all the time. This is difficult for most of us. Awareness of the presence and activity of grace among us is the beginning of being able to listen to secrets.

When there is much that distracts us from listening to others, our first step is to *become aware of ourselves*. To listen well, we must be clearly aware of ourselves and know who we are and what we feel as thoroughly as possible. This requires that we be honest with ourselves. We tend to err on one side or the other of acknowledging to ourselves who we are—we see ourselves as less than we truly are and, alternatively, as more than we are—and seldom perceive with the clarity and honesty we need to see ourselves as we truly are with both limitations and gifts.

Further, lack of awareness of ourselves means that underlying concerns for ourselves emerge as we listen and prevent us from hearing someone else fully. We get distracted internally and, without self-awareness, we allow the distractions to take us away from the speaker and their confession. Vigilant self-awareness enables us to recognize any shift in our focus and enables us to return to the speaker.

We must be aware of both our strengths and our limitations—*honestly* aware. For example, I should be aware of what is most likely to interfere with my listening carefully to someone. From one moment in time to another, from one day to another, our listening abilities change due to many circumstances. Limitations do not mean that we cannot listen at all, but that we must be aware of what limits our listening and build a more compatible circumstance for listening. Such limitations can also be dealt with through openness. "I am a bit distracted right now and I want to hear what you have to say." "Let me deal with this first. Then I can listen better." Why not confess these moments? Think about *your* answer to that question.

All of us are affected, to some degree, by physical circumstances. When we are ill, tired, or uncomfortable for other reasons, our listening is not at its best. Give yourself permission to notice these distractions. At other times our limitations may be emotional, when we have left something unfinished or a significant relationship is troubled. Such limitations do not have to dictate that we cannot listen at all, but may lead us to agree on another time when, hopefully, we will be able listen more carefully—when we can be more fully present.

Other times, when someone's need to be heard seems profound, awareness of our limitations can tell us we have to work harder to focus and listen better. Our limitations do not have to determine whether we can listen. Our limitations do need our recognition and our response. Having awareness of what distracts us from listening helps us listen better.

Physical limitations and personal distractions are not the only interference in listening ability. All of us have some topics or issues that we just cannot listen to. I have the picture in my mind of the pastor who put his hands over his ears when the subject of sex was mentioned. (He just did what others felt!) This is another area in which we need awareness. We must know which topics immediately cause us to tune out or turn away—issues that make us uncomfortable. We have issues that reflect our prejudices, which bring out our tendencies toward judgment or remind us of our inadequacies. The listener with high levels of awareness will be more likely to stay with the secret teller. When we are in the midst of listening we may discover a new "turn off" that we had not before realized. Becoming aware of this new discovery in real time will help our listening in the long run as well as at the moment.

The Character of One Who Listens Well

Feeling secure within oneself and within one's community contributes to effective listening. When we communicate that we are comfortable with others and open to hear whatever they bring, those who need someone to hear their secrets are able to speak. The person who wants to reveal a secret needs a listener who can be trusted—trusted to hear carefully; trusted to not judge, condemn, or reject the teller or any other persons involved in the secret; trusted not to tell others the secret. The key ingredient is *respect* for the secret keeper and the secret. The listening is focused on the teller's feelings. The listener's feelings must be put aside for now.

Be willing and able to tolerate expressions of anger. The anger will not likely be directed at you, nonetheless, for many of us anger is difficult to listen to and receive, regardless of where it is directed. This is not a time to take the anger personally, even though our first inclination is that any anger expressed is focused on us. *Trustworthiness* communicated to the teller allows the teller to express anger and to believe the secret and its feelings are safe with the listener.

Openness is an essential for those who listen to shameful secrets—an openness that includes the willingness to hear painful secrets and to allow the secret keeper to decide not to tell. Openness also includes a degree of "unshockability." At the heart of openness is the communication of respect for the person and for the secret that is told.

Openness is also a general attitude and stance. It allows for some recognition of diversity among people. People have experiences that are unfamiliar to the listener. Openness communicates readiness to grow and learn on the part of the listener. Being open is about how we are.

Being heard is like being received with a warm welcome, an offering of hospitality. The listener graciously acknowledges the speaker's presence. The listener offers the secret keeper a "comfortable place to sit" and some "refreshment."[7] A true welcome receives the words spoken and the meanings behind, underneath, and even concealed within the words. Being heard is like being received after a long, lonely, dusty, and difficult journey.

Hospitality is one way to think about openness in being able to hear confessions of secrets. Hospitality has to do with how we receive others—a welcoming stance in life and church relationships. The practice of communicating "I see you" to others reflects openness and hospitality. We meet and greet people *where* they are and *how* they are. We speak in ways that demonstrate the inclusiveness that welcoming requires. We allow ourselves to hear views that are different from our own. This kind of openness can affect our judgment of others. An attitude of hospitality assures secret holders that we can hear their shame and pain. People will get to know these things about the listener. Our *living hospitably* is instrumental in convincing secret holders to speak.

The minister who demonstrates a leadership of *servanthood* also encourages confession of shameful secrets. Rather than being a leader who "stands over" those who follow, this leadership that embraces the humility of servanthood expresses the warmth of hospitality and accessibility of openness as Jesus demonstrated in washing the feet of the disciples (John 13:5-10).

Keeping the Speaker as the Focus

Our ability to keep our focus on someone to whom we listen has to do with who we are. We think we are listening to one another, but much of the time we simply are not. We are nearby when someone is speaking. We are not talking at the same time (sometimes). We may be looking the speaker in the eye. We may be nodding our head in agreement or frowning sympathetically. But how much do we actually hear—even when we demonstrate our apparently attentive behavior and make some kind of response? Sadly, those people who are closest to us often receive the least of our listening.

We may hear the words spoken and be able to repeat them verbatim—or not. Being able to repeat the words someone speaks does not necessarily mean that we know the meaning the speaker intended. Nor does it indicate that we have truly heard the speaker. Listening is an art. According to one author, Michael P. Nichols, listening is a "*lost* art."[8] Listening is active and hard work, and listening is not the same as passively being present while someone is speaking.

When we think we are listening, we are too often racing ahead to think about the next thing we will say. We prepare to give the speaker some answer to the situation being described. We get busy thinking of questions we can ask about what the speaker is saying. While we do all of this planning we do not *hear* the situation being described. We fail to receive and respect the speaker's feelings. The more difficult something is for us to hear, the more readily we run away in our minds and then in our responses. In the midst of all we are doing, we may begin to evaluate the speaker and what we hear from him or her.

As we listen to another person, we think about what we will do next in our day. We may become anxious as we listen and attempt to signal the person that we are finished listening. We preoccupy our minds with other things we need to do. The list of what we do when we act like we are listening to someone is long. With all or any of these internal activities, the heart of what the speaker says is lost to us. Their relief at having spoken about their struggle is lost for the speaker because they, deep down, recognize that they were not *received*. Another possibility is that before they speak their deepest secrets, they realize they will not be heard and they stop speaking.

Recently I attended a luncheon and was seated next to a pastor I had not previously met. I *thought* we were getting acquainted. We engaged in a conversation in which he told me about himself. I began to respond to what he had said, and after just a few moments, he pulled out his cell phone and began to check his messages. I stopped speaking in the middle of a sentence, and he didn't even notice. We never resumed our conversation. It is so easy not to listen. This man certainly is not alone in the act of turning to a nonpresent person rather than keeping his focus on the person present. Technology triumphs as a new barrier to listening. If he had to deal with an emergency that took his attention, saying so would have felt quite different from being ignored.

The speaker must remain our focus. When the focus shifts to one's self, either internally or externally, or to something else happening nearby, or to others via text messages, we lose the speaker's message or distort it by our own interests. We move the speaker to the periphery and our "stuff" takes center stage. These are all things we must avoid if we want to listen well. *Every part of listening is harder to do when we listen to a secret.*

Speakers notice our "ways of not listening." Speakers are surprisingly conscious of our inattention; so the ways mentioned that we use to avoid hearing stand in the way of speakers being able to confess their shameful secrets.

Listening and Not Judging

When we truly hear, we do not just get the words, but we also get the person. The listener who really hears the speaker gives the speaker an experience of being honored, as the listener gives respect to the words spoken. The listener values the secret keeper. This is in contrast to being half listened to, which clearly does the speaker dishonor in its neglect of what the speaker says and, consequently, its neglect of *who* the speaker is and of the pain that is spoken.

When we hear some secrets, they immediately call forth our evaluating and judging selves. We feel anger toward described experiences of mistreatment and injustice. We feel frustration about the teller not doing what we think could have been done, "Didn't you tell your parents?" "Why didn't you talk to someone when this happened?" "What you did was wrong." Our judgment becomes judgment of the teller. These responses do not help the teller. We get judgments off our chests when they are spoken. We abandon the secret, and its importance is lost. The secret's confession fails to become an avenue to grace and healing. Instead, these responses help us distance ourselves from the speaker. *We* are not vulnerable.

Listeners also feel compelled to judge perpetrators who have played a role in some secrets. "What a louse!" a listener may exclaim with righteous indignation. It is not ours to take on the anger and frustration, the hate and fear, or even the pain of the secret keeper or for the secret keeper, but it is ours to hear their feelings. "You felt helpless," is a response that honors the feelings of the secret keeper. This is more useful than an expression of our own outrage, "How could she have done that?"

There is another problem with judgment. When we are judgmental during other times—like in our preaching and teaching—we set up an expectation within the secret keeper that he or she would be judged if he or she tells their secret. Pastors may feel they ought to judge many of the things people keep as secret. This means that we close some doors for people who may want and need to speak about a secret. Sometimes we just can't help ourselves and have to take a righteous stand against some things. We need to take such stands with awareness that we may be closing some doors. Those doors, had they remained open, perhaps would have provided an opportunity for someone to confess their secret and begin to move from shame into reconciliation, renewal, and wholeness.

The difficulties of listening make it important for those who would hear shameful secrets to learn how to listen well. What do we do to prepare ourselves to listen well under the difficult circumstances posed by hearing a shameful secret?

Being Able to Hear the Outrageous Secret: It's Not Just the Facts

We must be prepared to hear *anything*. People keep secrets because of the secret's significance—what the secret has meant to the keeper; how the keeper experienced the secret. After hearing a secret, response should be given more to the experience of the secret keeper, and not so much to the facts of the events involved in the kept secret.

Secrets are outrageous for different reasons. Some secrets are outrageous for their awful content. It is hard to believe that such a thing could *ever* have happened! We are incredulous. We easily doubt the veracity of the secret teller, if we do not remain aware of ourselves. Doubting the truth of the events described diminishes the secret kept and the person telling the secret. No matter how outrageous, the secret must be received "as is," as it is *felt*, as it is *told*.

We may become concerned about believing what is told to us because of the age of the secret teller. Age may be an outrageous factor as we listen. We may immediately doubt a young child, son, or daughter of a church leader or a colleague in ministry who tells us a shameful secret about parental abuse. "How could this be true? I know your parents, and they are good people." If we do not speak these words, they still may be in our minds.

At the other end of age, are we ready to believe the nursing home resident who reports abuse, whether it was carried as an untold secret from their childhood or a more recent abuse experienced in the nursing home—at the hand of a staff member or family member? Can we trust the memory of someone who is so old? The age of the secret keeper influences how or even whether we accept confessions. Age should not become a barrier to our believing the speaker or to our reception of them as loved by God.

Some secrets are also outrageous when they do not seem like "such a big deal." The secret keeper reports having been deeply affected by events that the listener might evaluate as insignificant. Remember Shirley's secret of the boys in town who molested her? It sounds like they just "felt her up," as we used to say. "Doesn't that happen to *every* girl at some time or another? What's the big deal? Why did this become such a major issue in Shirley's life?" When the secret is told, it is important that the secret and the teller not be judged in any way. Some questions we want to ask are not helpful: "Why didn't you tell your mother?" "Did you tell the boys no?" "They didn't really *hurt* you, did they?" *These questions carry implied judgment.* The speaker hears, "You should have..." even when it isn't spoken. We have other questions we think of asking, like (for Shirley) "Why did you let the boys do that?"

All of the questions mentioned have probably existed for the secret keeper for some time. They will come out when the keeper reaches a safe point of disclosure. None of these responses are appropriate because they miss the meaning and depth of the secret teller's experience. Always the meaning for the secret keeper must be what we hear and value above all of our logic and reasonableness.

Those who have kept secrets need to be their own judges of what they are able to do and when. Their secrets must be freely shared and never sought after. In every instance of which I have heard the revelation of a secret, it was a surprise to the listener who received it. Sometimes, however, after the secret keeper speaks, there is a sense of recognition when the listener makes some connections from past conversations or observations. The hearer would never have been able to put the pieces together, but after hearing the secret, the pieces become apparent, and the whole picture makes sense.

Response after Hearing

Careful listening extends to the listener's response. After a secret is told, the speaker may ask the question, "Now what do you think of me?" (This question is repeated word-for-word by many who confess secrets.) Even when this question is not voiced, it is lying right under the surface of the moment. This question reflects the shame that has held the secret. In confessing, the secret teller is exposed. The shame is revealed. You, the listener, see something quite new about the teller. The image and understanding you had of the person may be radically altered by the information you receive. This is a difficult moment, whether this question is asked or not. Spoken or unspoken, do not allow the question of what you think of the speaker to hang there.

The nature of your relationship to the teller determines what kind of response to give after hearing the secret. Affirmation of the continued positive regard you hold for the person should be made explicit. Clear and repeated affirmation of the secret teller is necessary.

Several other responses are important at this point. First, express the honor felt at being told the secret. Express appreciation for being trusted to hear the secret and all of the feelings involved in it, including reassurance that the story will be kept secret by you and not told to anyone else.[9] Reassure the speaker that you are willing and ready to hear more about the secret, when the person wants to tell more or to review or what was said. This could be the time to tell the keeper that, often, when secrets are told, the secret keeper will want to talk about it more with the one who heard the secret. This information is especially important when you are the only one who heard the secret. Invite the teller to speak with you again. Set a time to meet. Wonder out loud if there is more the speaker wants to say right now.

If you feel that dealing with the secret confessed is beyond your abilities, be prepared to suggest the possibility of talking to another professional and be sure to have someone in mind as a referral. Here accurate self-assessment is important. Do not underestimate what you can deal with, any more than you would overestimate it.

Conclusion

Preparing to hear confessions of shameful secrets is demanding. We can see the rewards when we recognize that just in telling a kept secret, a person who has carried this secret as a burden starts to feel healing begin—just in telling and being heard! We see how some people *prepare* to tell, how others just *happen* to tell and still others tell when an occasion *releases* the secret—when a door is opened.

Sometimes people make several attempts to "test the water" in order to see if the secret will be heard and they will not be rejected. Communicating in your welcome that you will hear a secret with respect and openness, with expressions of God's grace and boundless love, makes telling the healing event it promises to be. We see many ways we can be prepared to hear secrets. These ways of being in relationships communicate openness to receiving confessions of secrets.

Confessing a secret is moving toward peace and wholeness, an experience of God's grace as well as healing. Telling is a step toward renewal in life and in community. When a part of one's life is a source of shame and is kept hidden, it is unlikely that the keeper of the secret will experience peace, renewal, or wholeness. Experiencing wholeness requires acceptance of self. What is kept shamefully secret impedes self-acceptance. Peace cannot comfortably dwell in one's life when shame rules. Faithful listeners can participate in the secret keeper's movement toward wholeness by receiving what was stored as shameful.

Chapter 2

Listening Is Not Trading Secrets

Keeping Confidentiality and Maintaining Ethical Boundaries

Introduction

Whenever we listen to someone telling something that is painful, we face a temptation to tell the speaker something from our experience that will demonstrate that we understand. We want them to know we hear what they are saying, and one of the closest routes to letting them know is to tell them *our* story that is related to theirs, or some story that seems connected (that we may have heard confidentially) from another person. In other words, we want to say, "me too," or "I *know* because I have faced this before."

People do not want to feel they are alone in their experience, and we are ready to accommodate. We hear their struggle. We sense their pain. We may go so far as to claim that we "feel their pain." We are relieved to be able to make and communicate this connection. This behavior allows the *listener* to feel better, but how does it feel to the speaker? The listener says, "Let me prove to you that I understand."

Once I feel I have accomplished this, *I* am more comfortable, that is *until* the speaker turns to further explore my story!

This chapter deals with our temptations related to being listeners to the painful confessions of secrets. What do we hope to accomplish by sharing related stories? There are always dangers when we are tempted to tell our own stories or a story we have heard from another person. At the center of our defenses is the vulnerability we experience when we listen to others' secrets.

We know they are being vulnerable when they tell us what they have held in shame. We must realize that we also are vulnerable when we listen. Efforts to tell our own stories or the secrets of others are ways to avoid our own vulnerability as we listen. Telling our stories gives us control in the situation. Taking charge enables us to avoid feeling vulnerable.

When we have heard others' secrets, we become responsible for keeping what has been said in confidence. The one who listens must be trusted to keep to her- or himself what has been said. There are some exceptions to this rule. The person who hears others' secrets must keep up-to-date with regard to denominational expectations and state laws. Mandated reporting may be required when a secret involves endangering lives of others or crimes that have been committed or when the speaker is a danger to him- or herself.

We must be committed to keeping confidential secrets others have shared. We have to recognize the essential nature of keeping secrets others have shared. Pastors have particular temptations in this regard since there is so much told that would make good sermon illustrations. To alleviate the tension of being the repository of shameful secrets, some clergy find relief by sharing with their spouse secrets they have been told. Both of these behaviors must be seriously reevaluated. When we receive something so personal, so powerful, as kept secrets, the person confessing must be confident that we will keep their secrets to ourselves. We must consistently act responsibly in regard to what we hear.

Confidentiality works more effectively when the faith community recognizes the need for a context that favors confidentiality. Both organizations and families are often far from being contexts that sustain confidentiality when individuals within the community perpetuate gossip and share freely what they hear. Persons in ministry have the hard work of creating a sense of value of confidentiality, so that a context for it can be built and supported in the community. We need to clarify within the community distinctions between confidentiality and secrecy.

Part I: Making Ill-Informed Connections: No "Me Too"

In order to offer necessary care while receiving a shameful secret, I recognize the importance of making some connection with the speaker. It is not enough that I know I have made this connection, but I want very much for the speaker to acknowledge that I have made a connection with what they have said. This is a familiar human tendency. While we listen to another person we are sorting through our own experiences, trying to see where we have a connection with them. This dynamic is true in personal as well as professional experiences. The importance of these connections may be a subconscious reason that we often are more comfortable with people who have backgrounds similar to our own. We expect that we have a better chance of finding connections with them, forgetting that there is much in human experience that spans locations, ages, and cultures, wherein we could find surprising connections.

It's Not about You

How do we go about listening to others' confessions and avoid the powerful ways in which we listen to what they say and also see it as about us? Another way to put this question would be, "How do I keep my focus on the speaker?" That doesn't sound so difficult, unless the person speaks about something that touches your life or raises one of those issues (common in secrets) that you cannot face, like death, sex, suicide, or violence. When these issues emerge from the speaker, we have temptations to get them to stop talking about what *we* want to avoid. We know how to do that. We focus on our own experience, our own secrets or the secrets of others who may have tried to speak with us about similar issues. We ask questions about what interests us in what has been said. We want to go anywhere but there!

Sometimes the connections we make in our minds are reminders of secrets others have told us. These relationships offer us ways to understand the speaker. The trouble is that when we make such connections, we tend to dwell on what we know from our previous experience and fail to focus adequately on what makes *this* speaker's story unique. Because of this failure, we do not see the particularities of what this speaker says, which means we cannot fully understand their experience. We allow our experience, which may be similar to the speaker's (never the same), to overwhelm the speaker's account and take center stage. We stop listening to the speaker's account and reflect on what we know or what we have heard some other time. Our response is bound to be at least somewhat off base in relation to their confessions because we have taken such a journey while they speak.

The Unhelpful "Me Too" Connection

We want to join with someone in their struggle; and when we can say "me too," we think our joining with them is made real to them. This tendency to seek connection in our experience even leads us to interrupt others so we can demonstrate that we made a connection. We can't wait until they have finished what they are saying. Actually, we sometimes think of what we have to say (from our experience) as embellishing and clarifying their story—even when they have not completely told us everything. In effect, what we are doing is shifting the focus from them to the story we have. Maybe I am the only one who does this, but I doubt it.

In my first ministry experience, post seminary, I had a powerful experience of this temptation and recognized its disaster as it unfolded.[1] In this experience the mother of a teenage boy in the youth group with which I was working came to see me to talk about her son. She was experiencing some struggles with his behavior at home. Her description sounded familiar to me from the start. I felt a connection with my own experience with my brother. I offered my discovery, "He sounds just like my brother!" Her face lit up as she eagerly asked me how my brother had turned out.

Crash! At that time, my brother's life was not going that well. What could I say to her? I have no idea what I did say. I know I was horrified that I had offered false hope. (The look on her face held such expectation!) How could I rescue that moment without lying or distorting the truth? I had put myself in a bind and could not offer her a helpful response. My desire to let her know that I understood what she was saying came directly from my own insecurity in the role of helping her—wanting to please and not wanting to fail. Ultimately, I did not want to be vulnerable.

What I learned from this painful experience was the importance of allowing my experience to help me hear what she was saying and not letting it determine what I heard. This distinction is important. Connections with my own experience may prove helpful to me in my own reflections on her situation, but will *not* be helpful to tell the secret keeper.

When someone is confessing a shameful secret, the tendency to tell my story may be a way for me to avoid hearing his or her confession. When I take control of the conversation, I don't have to hear someone's uncomfortable secret.

Part II: Building a Context for Confidentiality

Dealing with confessed secrets raises particular concerns about confidentiality. The requirement of confidentiality reaches beyond the minister's authority. Both denominational and state laws require confidentiality and place limits on its practice under specified circumstances. The difficulty for those in ministry leadership lies in the differences that exist from one state to another and from one religious body to another. These distinctions are further complicated by the changes that frequently are instituted by church and by state. Keeping informed is necessary. Most denominational web sites provide information about their rules and expectations.[2] These include important distinctions made between ordained leaders and laypeople functioning in leadership. Those who serve in nondenominational or independent settings are further challenged to design their own rules on boundaries and necessary procedures within the church for their enforcement. State laws bind nondenominational or independent churches as well.

The Importance of the Context for Confidentiality

Beyond any rules of morality, the minister has a responsibility to create a *context* for confidentiality that is expected and shared within the community by pastor and parishioner alike. This means that *responsibility for keeping confidentiality cannot itself be a secret*. We must talk openly about keeping confidentiality within the community. We hold the expectation that those in ministry will keep confessions confidential, but this expectation needs to be valued throughout the entire community. Confidentiality is a way of community that enables the maintaining of relationships of care and trust. Confidentiality is valued and respected throughout the community. Communities have many lapses of confidentiality, so we face significant barriers to success in building a community where secrets confessed can remain secret with those who have been told, and a sense of trust runs throughout the community.

Support for the expectation that their secrets will not be exposed is reflected in the manner in which the pastor does ministry. Many pastors tell stories about people's struggles in sermons and refer to their issues in public prayers. Even if the preacher does not give names, people in the community often can place the story and identify the cast of characters. Alternatively, they may hear a story that is similar to their own experience and become embarrassed that they are being exposed. It is impossible for those in ministry to know when there is someone in their church related to a person from a former church whose story they tell. Interesting illustrations are not worth risking trust. Parishioners who hear another's story in a sermon, without affirmations of having permission to use the story, are not very likely to share a secret with the pastor who tells the story. They may think their story will be next.

The use of peoples' stories in sermon illustrations can be done, but *only* when permission has been sought and given, and the approval for the use of the story is stated by the minister. "I have asked those involved if I could use this story and I was given permission to do so." It is not necessary that names be used in order for approval to be sought. When names are used it should be stated that approval was given for this as well.

Preachers may feel that their families are good subjects for sermon illustrations, but this practice may undermine the effectiveness of a context of confidentiality. If the pastor can share such intimate things about her or his family, what does that say about the foundation of confidentiality needed for the church? I have heard too many demeaning stories about ministers' families. Again, sharing when permission has been sought, received, and asserted in the sermon is a different matter.

Sometimes prayer requests are made with the expectation that the names of the ones in need of particular prayer will be shared with others in the congregation. In other instances, prayers are requested and anonymity is sought—maybe the pastor does not even know who requested the prayer. When a significant number of prayer requests are submitted, it can become a problem for the pastor to be able to remember which are to remain confidential and which may be made public. This situation requires extra sensitivity and effort on the pastor's part to maintain confidentiality.[3]

Limits of Confidentiality

The people need to know the limits of confidentiality for those in ministry. State laws determine or mandate what must be told when a pastor or a lay minister hears something in confidence. For example, any charge or account of child or elder abuse *must be reported* to proper authorities. This may be one of the more universal laws. Ministers are also required to report any threat of doing harm to self or others. These are matters requiring urgent attention and cannot just be dismissed. The minister hearing a story involving child or elder abuse of any kind cannot make it her or his responsibility to discern the truth of the allegation. That investigation or discernment is not appropriate in the role of ministry. Nor is it appropriate for the person in ministry to make a judgment about the truth of the allegation. It is also a bad idea for the minister to choose to confront any alleged perpetrator.

When a perpetrator confesses their abuse of another person, the minister's role may include how she or he can provide caring ministry to the abused person. The role of the minister could take the form of being available to that person. It would not be necessary to go to the person and report what you had been told, but to visit them with an openness to hearing and receiving whatever they might share. The minister demonstrates openness to listen by being available.

Perhaps reporting, in the particular cases mentioned, will not have to be done by the minister who hears, but the person reporting can be encouraged and enabled to tell authorities themselves. Support to tell can make it possible for the person to report to the authorities what they have told you. Such advocacy could involve the minister taking the person to the authorities or going with them. This is not a matter of forcing someone to do such reporting, but a matter of our sustaining them in their choosing and acting. When the person says they will report it and fails to follow through, the minister must do the reporting.

The person confessing a secret could also be a perpetrator whom we would encourage to go to authorities him- or herself. Our willingness to stand with the perpetrator when they face authorities may be an important gift to them. It may be the factor that will enable them to reveal what they have done to others in order for justice to be done. A perpetrator may feel the importance of confessing their crime in order to be forgiven—making restitution may be meaningful for one who chooses to confess to a minister.

Who You Are in Ministry Informs the Context

Lebacqz and Driskill offer a perspective on ethics for those in ministry, "Several decades ago, ethics was largely understood as a matter of rules and principles. Today, commentators stress character and virtue."[4] Instead of coming up with the correct list of rules for ethics in ministry, focus on the character of those who do ministry may be more helpful. Lebacqz and Driskill further state, "The creation of genuine community may be at the core of all good clergy ethics."[5] The character of the minister and the health of the community are foundational in the practice of ethical ministry.

Ronald Richardson, focusing on the health of congregations, offers excellent perspectives on some important dimensions of character for leadership in ministry.[6] These are particularly relevant when we think about the character necessary within the context of confidentiality. Foundational to all that he suggests is *self-awareness.* First, he names "the less anxious presence" that offers a level of calmness enabling others to also be less anxious. Being less anxious requires that we know what will set us off into anxiety. Someone wanting to confess a shameful secret will be much more likely to talk with someone who is present in a nonanxious way. Being less anxious helps to establish a context for confidentiality as well as signaling to persons with secrets that you will not be undone by hearing their secret.

In addition, a nonanxious presence requires a solid sense of *self-esteem*, not arrogance, but a careful self-assessment of strengths and limitations, resulting in a confident presence. Confidence is not the same as arrogance. Arrogance can easily turn the confessing of a secret aside. It involves belief that one can solve the speaker's problems, which is not what the secret keeper needs. Rather than arrogance, honest humility is a helpful stance that includes accurate self-assessment.

Second, Richardson sees *being curious* and seeking to understand as essential. With this characteristic, the minister demonstrates interest in the other rather than presenting them with answers. The expectation is that the minister will be learning something from paying attention to the other, their circumstances, and what they have to say. This characteristic requires that the person in ministry will allow the person the *space* necessary to confess their story. Curiosity does not require asking questions as much as allowing room for the person to continue speaking. Curiosity about the person speaking and their confession helps us avoid interjecting our stories.

Rather than responding with questions out of curiosity, my tendency is to respond tentatively with, "I wonder (about what you just said)." Simply stating, "I did not understand what you just said (about...)." Not following this up with a question reflects a tentative stance. Being tentative reveals my recognition of being a human being, which means I am limited in what I can see and know.

Third, Richardson calls for "objectivity." I do not agree with that label but I think what he describes is very important. What he describes as objective I see as *balance* rather than an autonomous response that conveys we are either way ahead of the speaker or want to get out of the way of the speaker's emotions. When we are able to be present to others' expressions of pain, anger, grief, despair, and fear, for example, we are able to represent the character that is needed to offer care for them as they approach their deepest shame and present it to us for our response. Our approach with balance enables the secret keeper to feel less fear about what will happen if or when they tell. Balance keeps us from being autonomous extremists who look for what we can judge. It helps us see different dimensions of what is told rather than the narrowness that would, more likely, call for judgment.

Another characteristic in the minister that will contribute to creating a context for confidentiality is being one who *communicates hope.* Persons needing to confess secrets sometimes have not done so because they have not seen hope beyond telling the secret. One pastor was just beginning his ministry in a church that he and the congregation were seeking to grow. They had gone through a frustrating period of declining membership and participation. "Pastor Sidney" suggested that they provide weekly fellowship meals for the church community. The people told him that no one would come. They had no hope for his idea. What he did provides a model that can be used in other circumstances—even with individuals who see no hope. He took the stance of carrying hope for them until they could own it themselves. They did have the weekly meals. The church did grow.[7] In time the people carried the hope for their church themselves. This is a powerful image for individuals confessing secrets. Sometimes the very reality of a minister holding hope for them contributes to their being able to tell.

Members of the community will be able to see these characteristics in the person of the minister in many functions within the community of faith. The congregation perceives that the community is where confidentiality is highly valued.

Part III: Boundaries

Each person in ministry, at every moment in ministry, needs clear awareness and constant maintenance of boundaries. This requirement becomes especially true in the hearing of confessions. Too many persons entering ministry are given boundary-keeping advice that focuses only on *protecting themselves* in their ministries. This is not what I choose to emphasize here. My concern is for boundaries that secure and protect the secrets confessed to ministers and the persons who bravely confess those secrets.

We have already considered issues related to boundaries when we looked at how tempting it is to intrude our own stories into the stories of persons confessing their secrets. Boundary issues include avoiding the use of secrets in sermons as illustrations or in any other way that exposes a secret or secret teller.

How we see boundaries is further complicated by their deep-rootedness in the American or Western cultures. Here boundaries assume excessive valuing of autonomy.[8] We are in need of a balanced understanding of boundaries that participate in our caring for others. The importance of boundaries in this discussion about secrets is most concerned with the protection of persons with secrets and not with those who hear their secrets. Of course, ministers need to have boundaries to ensure that they are not overwhelmed by secrets they hear confessed, for example. Boundary keeping is not the responsibility of the person confessing the secret, but of the person who offers ministry and who is the receiver of confessions.

Complicating the issue of boundaries, when we deal with secrets kept, is the struggle some people with secrets may have in keeping their own boundaries. Their boundaries may be troubled by the burden of shame with which the secret is bound. They have done well keeping boundaries around their secrets as they are hidden, but the origins of their secrets may create for them some confusion about maintaining boundaries and their rights to keep them. Many shameful secrets have to do with boundaries of the secret keeper having been disrespected or violated.

People with shameful secrets can become targets for ministers who may disregard concerns of behaving ethically. We want to think we in ministry are beyond misconduct, but the many incidents of pastoral misconduct create discouragement about this belief.[9] Parishioners are never responsible for misconduct by persons in a ministerial role. The concept of consenting adults does not apply because of the unequal power differential between minister and parishioner.

We do not know how many clergypersons indulge in clergy sexual misconduct.[10] These often are well-kept secrets. An Internet search for "clergy sexual misconduct (or abuse)" leads to results of many studies and reports. For example, Baylor University conducted research from 2008-2009 including 3,559 respondents leading to a conclusion that "there are, on average, 32 persons who have experienced CSM [clergy sexual misconduct] in their community of faith." Their research included a broad spectrum of Christian denominational groups and Jewish affiliations. They considered congregations of 400 congregants as average.[11] Other research reported differing results. The statistics cannot be considered as conclusive. What seems apparent is the presence of far too much clergy sexual misconduct and far too little disciplinary response to it.

A further boundary issue for the minister seeking to establish a context of confidentiality is the need to be aware of the dynamics of becoming part of a negative triangle. This happens when he or she is engaged to listen to a complaint about or attack on someone else in the church or on the church staff. When we listen to "reports" about others, we become part of a gossip chain. No matter if we never say anything to anyone else about what we are told, we are perceived as being included in the secret process. Boundaries are violated. Trust is damaged. The ability of the people to believe in confidentiality in the community is damaged.

Instead of being a passive participant enlisted in the gossip chain, the minister must have the courage to refuse to listen. The minister could invite the speaker to go with her or him to talk directly to the person who is the focus of the gossip or complaint. This offer can be made with the sincere expectation that it can be done and that doing so will be helpful. This kind of invitation puts the minister's vulnerability at a high level. It also makes a significant contribution to developing a context of trust and confidentiality.

Conclusion

Confidentiality is essential when those in ministry receive confessions of secrets. Congregations that provide a context for confidentiality make it more possible that person with secrets will be able to confess them. Persons in ministry hold the possibility for the telling of secrets in their hands as they work with the people to establish such a context for confidentiality and demonstrate the characteristics of those who can honorably receive painful, shameful confessions and continue to care for each secret keeper. All of this is possible within our communities of faith as we are bearers of the grace of God to all the people and recognize our responsibilities in hearing and keeping secrets, and in reporting secrets to proper authorities when that is legally necessary. We hold the responsibility for recognizing and maintaining appropriate boundaries within our communities.

We have the opportunity to provide for the people the possibility of hope that lies beyond the secret confessed. This is made clear as we are able to be fully present with others, welcoming, receiving, and accepting them.

Chapter 3

The Pastor as the Bearer of Secrets

Introduction

Our work is not over when we have listened to others' secrets. We also become the ones who then bear the secrets that have been told to us, and some secrets are more difficult to carry than others. When and where do we get to put them down? How do we manage the burden they can become? What if, when we demonstrate that we are open to receiving shameful confessions, we get more and more secrets to carry? It could become enough to cause one to want to put up some barriers to prevent those in need from telling their secrets in the first place.

Some in ministry claim that prayer and faith in the sustaining power of God will always be sufficient. Others, who also have strong faith, might feel totally overwhelmed even as they faithfully believe and pray. A traditional alternative for male pastors has been to tell the secrets they have heard to their wives.[1] Some parishioners even have the expectation that what they have told the pastor has then been told to the pastor's wife, and look to her for feedback on their issue. For pastors, such an expectation from a parishioner is not appropriate encouragement to begin this practice. The expectation is not appropriate, but it does point to the need that pastors often feel to share the load.

Pastoral burnout may be to some extent rooted in the burdens carried from confessions people disclose. As we think about burnout, we also have to recognize that much of ministry tradition has failed to stress any significant importance on the pastor caring for himself or herself. If we receive these heavy burdens year after year and keep carrying them by ourselves along with all the other demands of ministry, we can expect burnout to visit us and even take us out of ministry.

We should recognize that there are other resources available to people in need and that we cannot carry everything ourselves. I think of the importance for everyone in ministry to accurately assess her or him self—neither overestimating nor underestimating what one is capable of handling.

In this chapter we will examine appropriate ways to deal with the burdens we end up carrying when we open ourselves to listen and receive the pains people need to confess. When we know we must keep secret confessions to ourselves, we might feel very alone bearing them as painful burdens. *We are not alone.* We can keep what we hear as confidential and act appropriately and professionally, while still finding support and sustenance.

Part I: How Much Can You Carry?

Where Are Your Limits?

One common way of discovering the limits to what one can bear in ministry has been actually reaching the point of burnout. This is not a good way to determine how much we can carry. In fact, finding out the limit to what one can carry is a mistaken approach altogether. Instead, persons in ministry can work to be self-aware and institute ways to take care of themselves on a regular basis—not only when they are desperate and approaching the end of their rope.

Persons in ministry sometimes have inclinations to overestimate what they can deal with in caring for others. They may take on situations and persons that they are not prepared to care for. The outcome is becoming (maybe rightly) overwhelmed and fearful—both for oneself and for the other in need of care and others related to them. Note that realizing this requires self-awareness. More recently, I have noticed how many people in ministry, rather than overestimate themselves, *underestimate* what they can do and, as a result they want to pass on any issue that comes to them for care to another professional. This can happen even before they have heard the whole story. Neither of these two self-assessments is helpful. Both rely on inadequate self-awareness. We need to know what we can do and have some courage to face the difficult issues people bring us, always knowing that we can make referrals as we continue or as the need arises. At times ministers underestimate their abilities because they are not familiar with the issues raised (or issues they *fear* will be raised) by the person confessing. When the minister feels unqualified to discuss sex and sexuality, for example, these are issues he or she will want to avoid. Instead, how about this; self-awareness helping you recognize this fearful lack of information and letting it lead you to study the issue and become better prepared to face it. Incidentally, any minister who does any premarital, wedding, or even divorce preparation needs up-to-date, accurate, and adequate knowledge about sex. When we consider confessions of shameful secrets, the ability to feel comfortable talking about sexual violence is essential.

What Can't You Carry?

Some secrets confessed are so traumatic and invasive for the one who hears them that they become extraordinary burdens to carry. The memories of what was told can reoccur for the listener. Reliving horrible accounts heard can become very disturbing. Here we see the need for a place to put the burden down—someone who could receive it from us. In addition, such torment for the minister may mean that there is some connection within her or his own experience. This aforementioned troubling arising from a parishioner's issue may indicate a need for counseling for the minister. It could be the minister's issue as well. If so, there would be a greater need for addition help with what he or she has heard confessed.

What you can't carry also includes what you should not carry according to denominational practices and state laws—including whatever you must report.

Helping Yourself

Part of what determines how much we are able to carry depends on how well we take care of ourselves. This is a touchy matter for many people in ministry. I remember having a little sign I made for myself when I was a teenager. It listed, from top to bottom: "God, Others, and Self." This was the order in which I was to give these issues importance, attention, and care. Once we have taken good care of our relationship with God and given others help or attention they may need, then maybe we will have a bit left over for ourselves. My list did not include "Family"; but it, too, would have come before "Self." This is the reality for many persons in ministry. The very last person to get any care or focus will be *myself*, and that often means there is little left. Bivocational ministers have added pressure regarding taking care of themselves. Their list of what comes before taking care of themselves has an additional level. The matter of taking care of one's self includes, rest, recreation, relationships, good nutrition, and exercise. Regular visits to dentist and doctor, not waiting for emergencies to do so, are also on the essential self-care list. These all take time. Who has the time for them? I am fond of using the airline instructions regarding self-care. The attendants always tell passengers, "Put the oxygen mask on yourself first and then help those who need help with theirs." They know what they are talking about. If persons in ministry fail to take care of themselves, they will not be *able* to care for others. When others always come first, there usually is no time for care of self. We have not had many models in ministry for good self-care. We have to begin becoming models for self-care.

Part II: Sources of Strength and Support

You Are Not Alone

Ministers may feel that, having been told secrets, they are to forever hold them without any revelation of their contents to anyone else. That is what confidentiality is about, isn't it? But there are other professional alternatives. Persons in ministry can find skilled persons to supervise their caring ministries—persons who will honor the confidentiality of the secrets told. Potential supervisors to serve as the pastor's confidant may be pastoral counselors, trained chaplains, or psychologists. Secrets may be shared with them in a professionally contracted arrangement, but even they do not need to hear specifics of names of persons involved. Their role can function to offer feedback on situations and on the minister's response to the confessing person. Supervisors should be persons who value faith issues and can be conversant in matters of belief and practices of faith. They can be contracted to work with a small group of ministry peers. Persons hostile toward or indifferent to faith issues will not be good choices. Supervisors should be carefully chosen and not selected when there is an emergency or because you saw an advertisement.

Accountability partners and peer groups can be other ways for persons in ministry dealing with confessed secrets to find strength and support beyond themselves. In every instance in which there are others with whom we share issues in ministry, we have to be assured of kept confidence. To have another pastor in town know and talk about a parishioner's secret in any public manner—even to a close friend—would be tragic. Boundaries must be made clear with anyone who is trusted to help share your burden. Boundaries of confidentiality are mutual and expected of you when you hear another's ministry concerns and struggles.

Ministers have resources available in seeking and practicing spiritual nurture, maintaining an active prayer life, and nurturing solid friendships beyond the faith community served and outside of their family. Participating in all of these supportive and sustaining activities provides strength for the journey in ministry.

The central issue regarding anyone with whom you seek support or guidance regarding confessions made to you is whether you can completely trust the person. There should not be any doubt or question about whether the person can be trusted. What you share should feel safe in their presence and practice.

Part III: Sharing Burdens

To some extent, carrying the burdens of confessed secrets is completely up to the minister. Maybe this seems to work fine if the church community is small enough. But community size cannot be the determining factor. The church Pastor Dan served was not a large church, but we saw that with one opened door, several secrets entered into his purview. Whether the women who spoke with him talked with him again soon after they confessed their secrets or not, the extent of their burdens could become a weight in his ministry. We also can imagine that the telling did not end with those few women and that perhaps others with shameful secrets discovered through that sermon (or others he preached) that he would be able and willing to hear what was shameful to them in their lives and held as secret. So, given a larger church, and some signal of openness to receive (welcome) shameful secrets, how much would a pastor discover?

How does the minister share the burden within the church? One role of ministry, often ignored, is the active and intentional preparation of lay ministers to share in the ministry of the congregation. Is that possible? Such ministry has been working effectively in the shape of Stephen Ministries since 1975.[2] In this ministry, lay people are formally trained to offer care to others in their church community. Alternative programs for preparing laypersons to offer care within a congregation are sometimes designed and developed within particular congregations. The workshop session offered in this book could provide a portion of preparation for laity intending to offer care for those who carry secrets.

Ministers need to be aware of the dangers of looking to persons within the congregation for personal support. The danger also applies to the pastor's spouse and family. The minister shares in intimacy with parishioners. They share personal issues and receive support, but this cannot be a two-way street in ministry.[3] This is a clear boundary issue, even when a person may be very trustworthy.

Part IV: Turning to Other Resources

Community Resources Are Options

Ministers need an in-depth familiarity with other resources available in their communities. For some, I suspect there may not be an awareness of Area Agencies on Aging. These agencies are everywhere and provide excellent and varied resources for older people in communities and congregations.

All twelve-step programs can be excellent resources and may even find your church to be a place where they would be welcome to hold meetings.

Therapists and counselors are available in most communities. The state licensed counselors and ministers need to be aware of this process and the credentials that should be expected for different levels of training and preparation.[4] Also be aware that the title "Christian Counselor" does not necessarily indicate a well-prepared counselor. Check the training and discover firsthand the attitudes and approaches of any counselor you might want to use for referral. Do not presume that a title or degree will give what it promises for your counselee in adequate care or counseling. Use caution and check out for yourself any person to whom you would trust someone who has been in your care. This means a personal interview. Request a conversation with a therapist for the purpose of making referrals. Any counselor should freely give such a consultation. Your agenda should include finding out what the person's training is, what their specialties are, and how they work.

In order to be prepared for making referrals, ministers need to have familiarity with counselors who specialize in marriage and family, sexuality, counseling children or adolescents, and grief counselors.

These are all areas in which ministers may need further help for particular people in their care.

Conclusion

Too many persons in ministry resist ways in which they could get help in carrying the burdens of ministry. They have not valued the potential of church laity to help share in the burden to be carried. This resistance means that laypeople have not received preparation for doing ministry that is needed and that many are capable of providing with preparation. An essential role of ministry is to provide such preparation, but pastors will not willingly share these burdens when they feel insecure, no matter how run-down or worn out he or she may be. From another perspective, we also have to address the congregants who refuse to accept any ministry from someone who is not the pastor. Neither the value of the minister nor the ministry is diminished when laypeople do ministry.

In chapter 5 the reader will find a chart depicting a spectrum ranging from autonomy to shame. In the middle we find balance that affirms both "I am limited" and "we need each other." Balance is where persons in ministry need to stand when they face the pressures and burdens they carry in tasks of ministry with additional weight of confessed shameful secrets. All the support and resources available will not be accessible to pastors who stand clearly with autonomy with the assertion, "You need me. I don't need you." Clergy burnout happens too often and leads to the end of too many valuable ministries. Without positive acceptance and affirmation of "we need each other," we deny the reality of both our community and our shared humanity.

Chapter 4

Is What You Hear the Truth?

The Role of Lying in Secret Keeping

Introduction

Deception is necessary in order to keep secrets. Shameful secrets are hidden with the use of deception through revised histories, evasions, silence, and outright lies. People keep secrets by hiding the truth in both active and passive ways. We lie to help us hide the shame that forces us to keep secrets and because we think it's easier than facing the truth. When we recognize the role of deception involved in keeping secrets, we may naturally question whether what we hear in the confession of secrets is actually true. Questioning whether what we hear is true is not meant to encourage our doubt, but to recognize what may be our inclination. Many shameful secrets may be, at first thought, unbelievable.

Where shame invades and demands a secret be kept, deception is a guard against discovery and a way for the secret keeper to remain safe. Deception as practiced by the holder of a secret may in fact assure her or his survival. This chapter seeks to avoid common dualistic thinking

63

about lying and honesty. Even as we recognize the role deception plays in keeping shameful secrets, we must be prepared to welcome what the secret keeper tells without judgment about their use of deception.

Part I: The Ambiguity of Lying

Neither lies nor truth are unambiguously wrong or right, as we have learned to think they are. Understanding truth telling and lying as opposites and absolutes does not serve us well. Life is more complex than such simplicity allows us. Lies may function to save our lives when we feel the life-threatening possibility that the exposure of shameful secrets carries. Persons of faith who want to affirm the absoluteness of truth could look to their scriptures.

In the Hebrew (Old Testament) scriptures, for example, in the story of Moses we see how his survival depended on deception—first, by the midwives who lied about his birth. The Egyptian midwives were ordered by Pharaoh to kill all Hebrew males when they were born. The midwives lied to Pharaoh and spared many babies' lives, Moses's included. Then Moses's sister and mother were able to remain in his life as caregivers, through deception, while he became part of Pharaoh's household. Could this patriarch of the faith have survived without deception?[1]

Yet, everyone knows that telling lies is wrong. We do not expect ourselves or others to make a practice of telling lies. However, lies are told whenever a secret is kept. To broaden this image, we need to think in terms of deception rather than a strict sense of the actual telling of lies. Hiding truth means deception, whether it is actively done in telling lies, or whether it is passively done in failing to tell the truth by keeping silence or by substituting misleading information, which hedges on outright lying. In keeping secrets we engage in telling lies, even to ourselves, sometimes to the extent that the truth may no longer be recognizable.

While I believe that the truth shall set us free, I also believe that the truth can be used as a destructive weapon. Truth can be used to do harm, sometimes unintentionally. We cannot accurately comprehend the roles of truth or lies when we see them as clear-cut and absolute, no matter how much we *want* them to be this way.

Kept secrets divide and diminish lives. Gifts are not put to full use because of the attention that must go into maintaining the secret. Division exists not only internally, inside the person, but also separates people from one another and limits sharing and the experience of genuine intimacy. Many lives lived within a cloak of secrecy are stunted rather than full and rich. Even when the secret keeper is able to fare well, we are left to wonder what the life lived without the hidden secret might have been. Rage related to the secret may smolder, hidden, throughout life and resentment may unexpectedly emerge, both taking a toll on any life lived in their company.

Most of us travel through our lives seeing ourselves as truthful people. To the contrary, all of us, with *few* exceptions, tell lies throughout our lives. Psychologist Paul Ekman quotes sociologist Erving Goffman, "No one really ever tells the truth, and it is not the truth that matters. What matters is that we follow the mostly unwritten rules of social life."[2] The rules to which Goffman refers encourage us to lie in order to be polite, those "little white lies." Lies are even expected under some circumstances, even while we see lying as negative. We *know* what the answer *should be* when asked whether someone's new outfit makes them look fat.

Truth is healing and helpful, however, I also want to expose lying as not being *completely* negative. Lying protects and serves us *under some circumstances*. In keeping secrets, lying becomes necessary, especially if keeping some secrets feels to us like the difference between survival and destruction. In some cases this feeling is valid—survival is at stake and the secret ensures it. Both truth telling and lying can function in the service of healing or doing harm, and sometimes both. Here we are concerned with the role of truth in telling secrets.

Part II: The Truth about Lies

Lying on the Way to Growing Up

Much to the dismay of parents and other adults, one of the methods of choice used by children to discover and assert their individuality is telling lies. Genuinely truthful children will at odd moments tell lies that achieve no particular purpose other than to permit them to know something their parents do not know. It is a means to establish one's own identity. "I will not let you know the whole truth about me, because I am on the way to becoming my own person."[3]

As children growing up, we find a variety of ways in which to begin to separate from the powerful adults in our lives. Children face adults in their lives who know so much that is a mystery to children. Being able to tell parents something that is not true gains the child a bit of territory of her own.

I do not affirm this role of telling lies; nor am I suggesting that telling lies is necessary in order to become one's own person, to grow up. I am not implying that young children make use of lying with awareness about becoming individuals. What I am describing is a use of lying that commonly takes place in human experience (at least in the predominant American culture) and has an outcome of children becoming separate individuals. Imagine the life of a child who is unable to keep anything from her or his parents. Put yourself in this child's place. How does this child grow up?

As children we learn to lie in order to avoid being punished when we have been disobedient or when we get into trouble. "I don't know how that got broken. It wasn't me." Lying serves us well in keeping us out of trouble—unless the lie is discovered and then the trouble compounds.

Learning to lie may come easily within families when children observe parents lying to other adults and catch them lying to the children themselves. Santa Claus, the Easter Bunny and, maybe, the Tooth Fairy are common lies parents tell children. Even good parents lie. Cautious parents may instruct children left at home alone to lie about being home alone. Do we want a child, who is alone, to tell a stranger the truth, that she is home alone? I would suggest that lies told to protect lives are not necessarily wrong.

Lies Hide Shame

More people than we ever would expect hide aspects of their lives. They hide alcoholism, drug addictions, criminal backgrounds, spouse and child abuse, sexual orientation, and marital affairs. They may hide family members and family secrets. Important aspects of their lives become lies. Who we perceive is not the whole person but only, perhaps, the tip of the iceberg. What they may experience is fear of isolation from their community because of their felt need to keep a significant part of their lives hidden. Even while secret keepers relate to others, they are isolated in the sense that they are preoccupied, on some level, with keeping their secret under wraps. It takes personal energy to live this way. It builds barriers between people, since the whole secret-keeping person cannot be available for relationships.

We force some people into this hiding when the church demonstrates judgment and disapproval of important issues in peoples' lives. When we do not affirm difficult choices mothers might make to relinquish their children for adoption, we can push them into lives of denying they gave birth and deception about their child's existence. The lives we see are denials of the entire truth. The women in Pastor Dan's church who experienced domestic violence felt trapped in marriages they could not leave or end because they understood that the church would judge that divorce, or leaving their marriages, was unacceptable.

A woman beaten by her husband may wear particular clothing and sunglasses that conceal her cuts and bruises or she may choose to remain home where no one can see her while her bruises or wounds are fresh. She cloaks herself in secrecy in order to save her family, her home, her dignity, her place in the community, her marriage, and her husband. There is a lot riding on keeping her secret. If she is asked directly about her sunglasses or why she isn't going out, she is likely to lie outright, creating a story different from the truth. "I ran into a cabinet door." This way she keeps the secret and with it her place in the community and as wife and mother.

Lying to Protect Others

While we think we are clear that lying is wrong, historically, lying has meant the saving of many lives in addition to lives in scripture. During our country's history of slavery, the Underground Railroad, which ushered many slaves to freedom, was a systematic trail of lying and deception. During wars on our home continent or abroad, dishonesty has often saved lives, won battles, and turned the tide of war. Spies discovered and disclosed enemy plans of action. The spies acquired these plans as they lived among the enemy and related to the enemy behind masks of deception. More unexpectedly, deception made it possible for women, disguised as men, to fight in many (if not all) of America's wars throughout history before their participation was officially sanctioned. The Civil War provides a historical view:

> Conservative estimates indicate that four hundred women served incognita with the Union Army; 250 with the confederacy. Mary Livermore, a Union nurse wrote in her memoirs, "Some one has stated the number of women soldiers known to the service as a little less than four hundred. I cannot vouch for the correctness of this estimate, but I am convinced that a larger number of women disguised themselves and enlisted in the service...than was dreamed of."[4]

This reality was omitted from the history I learned in school—a reality hidden during the Civil War and largely hidden since. It is a secret kept about what women can do.

During the Holocaust in Nazi Germany, many Jewish lives were saved by lies and deception when non-Jewish people hid Jews and helped them escape from danger. In these examples from world history,[5] not only did people break common standards about lying but also they put their own lives at risk in doing so. In these cases their lying endangered their own lives while they rescued others whose lives were threatened. We might conclude that when the truth puts others' lives at risk, the truth becomes the lesser value, secondary to preserving life.

Implicating Others

I have wondered in more recent years whether my mother's reluctance to tell her secret may have had some roots in concern about implicating her mother. She always spoke of her mother in glowing terms. According to my mother, Mom (what we called my grandmother) was perfect. Mother felt enormous guilt about having once, *just once*, talked back to her mother. Did Mom know about Pop's behavior? I wonder how she could *not* have known. If she did know, then why didn't she do something? That will remain a mystery. Did my mother suspect that Mom knew? She never hinted that her mother might have known.

From my perspective now, I understand that my mother had to trust her mother in order to survive. How else would she have had *any* safety in the context of their home? The idea of her mother knowing could not be allowed to enter her mind. I suspect others of her brothers and sisters had probably also been abused. It is difficult to believe that her mother would not have at least suspected.

Where secrets are concerned, often there are others who would be affected by the secret being exposed. These others are also, as in the case of Mom, those who might share in some guilt about the secret's existence. These others become a concern when the secret keeper is deciding whether to confess the secret.

Elaborate Protection

Deception only begins with self-deception, for others must be deceived in order to keep the secret. With the telling of her secret, my mother opened up for me new meaning of past events in our family.

When my older brother and I were babies and young children we lived on the first floor and mother's parents, Mom and Pop, lived upstairs in the same house. We were never permitted to go upstairs to visit when Mom was not there. What I remember being told about this rule was that Pop had "no patience with children," and we would just annoy him. This rule of not visiting with Pop alone was one of the most strictly imposed rules I can recall from my early childhood. This rule was based in deception. We *couldn't* know the truth.

Following the death of Mom, when I was seven years old, it took my mother only two years to get us out of that living arrangement that included Pop. But, in reflecting back, the move was probably completely engineered by using deception. My father and mother bought a piece of land in an adjacent state and my father, using every weekend, built a house for us. It was too small for Pop to live there with us. By default, he had to go somewhere else to live.

Mother's ability to accomplish this elaborate "escape" from Pop demonstrates some dynamics of secret keeping. For mother, as secret keeper, non-assertiveness became an art form. I am certain she never told Dad about her abuse by Pop. Her way of getting my father to build a house for us, which got us safely away from Pop, was done without ever telling my father what the move was actually about. The pretense was to get us "out in the country" where "we could have horses."

I loved horses, like many girls my age, and I also loved my school, my neighborhood, and my friends—*right where we were*. My parents were doing this—going to all this trouble to move—for me. It was my fault we were moving. I did and did not want to go. Mother's interest was probably focused on the protection of both my brother and me, but I had no clue about her true purpose. I was angry about the move and unable to express it.

As I heard my mother's secret, many years later, I finally understood the move for the first time and remembered the pain and anger I experienced because of it. How could I have resisted or complained openly, because the move was *for me?* When I heard mother's secret, I knew immediately that she had done a basically miraculous thing, getting my father to build a house, in order to get me (and my brother) away from potential abuse by her father. I am certain that she used deception and manipulation. It didn't matter how she did it, but it was clearly a way for her to save us from the threat of abuse, of which only she was aware.

Mother's correct assessment that my father had enough interest in and ability to provide our means of escape by actually building a new house for us, demonstrates her nonassertive skills. Nonassertive action does accomplish things, but it does so through manipulation and deception and not by means of direct action. Avoidance of being direct uses a lot of energy *and* effectively helps protect the secret.

Mother's way of escaping her father by taking this circuitous route reveals the workings of her lack of assertiveness. Why couldn't she just have told Pop to leave? My father's employer owned the house, so Pop had no proprietary rights there. In spite of his abuse of her for her whole childhood and youth, she still would not take such direct action to get him out of the house. Would it have meant that my father would have to find out the secret? Then what would have happened? Her deception was a delicate matter.

Mother was the oldest daughter in the family, so she probably had to overcome some internal, if not external, pressure for her to be the one to take care of Pop after Mom died. When we moved, Pop had to go somewhere else, and it was not by her request, choice, or demand. It was just a consequence of our moving to a new location where there was no room for him.

Part III: The Ambiguity of Truth

We want a clear-cut sense about lying and telling the truth. We want the rights and wrongs of both to be absolute. Dr. Diane M. Komp explores this territory and seeks to provide support for the clear division and the absolute necessity of telling the truth.[6] A lie is *never* appropriate, she asserts. If we have faith that is strong enough, we will entrust our telling of the truth to God and presume the outcome will be the best, and lives will be preserved. Lives will be saved since we have told the truth. Komp's expectation is that even in dire circumstances where lives were threatened and where lies might protect lives, everything will work out and lives will not be lost if the truth is told.

Komp challenges us (and our faith), but historically there is so much evidence of lives saved by deception. I am not willing to sacrifice *any* life for the sake of the sanctity of truth telling. I know some others will stand with Dr. Komp and disagree with my position on this point. We see truth from a different perspective. Like Dr. Komp, we want and expect the truth to be unambiguous, clear, and mostly self-evident. I wonder if it is even possible, with full intent, to be absolutely truthful at all times.

What I experience in an event is the truth of that event. But, when you have had the experience of the event along with me, your "truth" is more than likely to be different from mine. Which experience is true? If your experience and mine are different, what is the "real" truth about the experience? Is there a "real truth" about the experience? You might suggest that the real truth is what "actually happened." I would ask, "By whose account?"

We like to think that the truth is something concrete, factual, and able to be grasped, known, proven, and absolute. We even want it to be and imagine it to be unchanging. But this seems to represent a relatively small portion of the truth. The perspective of the one perceiving the truth affects the truth. Truth is different over time as the world goes through changes, as humanity grows and learns. "The sun revolves around the earth." "The earth is flat." These were once commonly held truths that we now know are not true. What lies ahead for us that we have yet to understand as "new" truths? What do these possibilities mean for the absoluteness of truth?

Complications of Truth Telling in Context

Telling the truth is complicated. For example, hearing a couple talk about some disagreements they had: Mrs. B. explains, "All he ever does to help out is to do the dishes!" Mr. B's version goes more like this, "I don't know what she is upset about. After all, I do the dishes." My reflection as I listen is that both are right. Their experiences of the same event are different and both are true. The perspective each brings to the same experience causes the difference. If they remain unable to see the reality of the other's experience, conflict will continue.

Telling the truth in relation to kept secrets is clearly related to context and perspective. There are appropriate and inappropriate times, places, and particular people with whom secrets can be shared. There are also appropriate ways to tell the secret. Secret telling adheres to the understanding of reality that we learn—the truth is context dependent. Secrets are related to life experienced from a particular perspective. When secrets are told, they come from a perspective guaranteed to be different from that of the person who hears the secret.

Shared Secrets Creating Community

Withholding truth can be understood as deception, but may be seen as quite appropriate under certain circumstances. A sense of belonging is enhanced when, within a group or family, there is an understanding that certain information belongs "just to us." Holding secrets "together" binds members of a group to one another, contributing to meeting an important human need for belonging. Secret societies such as fraternities and sororities and some religious organizations illustrate this benefit of secret keeping. There are secret handshakes and rituals that set those who belong apart from others and hold them together as an identifiable group.

Uneasiness with the Truth

As a further complication, we are sometimes uneasy with telling the truth. Sometimes truth is painful to face—internally or in the company of others. Sometimes it is so painful to face the truth that we, as human beings, have the ability to repress some truths and not even admit them to ourselves. *Repression* means placing experience in such a way in our memories that the memory is hidden from our selves. Repressed truth does not make it any less true than it would be as something we remembered without hesitation or delay.

Telling the truth to another sometimes creates uneasiness for the person listening as well as for those who struggle to tell. Most of us go to great lengths to avoid disturbing others, rocking the boat, or causing trouble. We have strong investments in others seeing us as "nice." Sometimes important truths go unsaid for the sake of keeping the peace—maintaining the equilibrium. "When people submerge their true feelings in order to preserve harmony, they undermine the integrity of a relationship."[7] In the long run what goes unsaid may end up destroying relationships—something that happens in too many marriages.

Couples getting married avoid telling one another significant things that they feel must be kept secret. We put off what needs to be said in order to heal, open up, or develop relationships because we fear disturbance that truth may bring. We do not expect relationships to be strong enough to hold the truth. Telling the truth takes courage. We struggle with facing change that some truths would create in our lives and in the lives of those around us. Not wanting to rock the boat has a lot of power, but the choice of peace keeping instead of truth telling means that we do not have the community God intends for us.[8]

We fear how others will react to what we tell—whether with rejection, judgment, anger, or disbelief. We would much prefer to keep things as they are, even when that means living with burdensome secrets and telling misleading lies and remaining uncomfortable. Even when it means that we live with isolation—avoiding, avoiding, avoiding. Even when deception builds barriers within a family or community, we avoid telling the whole truth. It is hard to tell the truth about anything that relates to what we hold with shame. We can see these dynamics when we look at Carrie's secret.

Carrie's Story

When Carrie and her husband, Bruce, got married, their sex life was as exciting as any teenaged couple could anticipate. At eighteen, their honeymoon period was everything they had imagined. They married without Carrie telling Bruce about her secrets from her childhood and earlier teen years. They did not recognize how much baggage they were taking into their marriage commitment.

As time passed, Carrie began to replay over and over in her head the abuse she had experienced as a child. She began avoiding sex with Bruce, giving excuses and making promises for another time. Carrie explains what happened:

> I became pregnant with our first child when I was 19 ½. That winter we were house sitting for some friends and had the absolute worst argument of our marriage to date. It was about sex, or more accurately, the lack of it in our relationship. Bruce was so patient and tried to understand when I would deny his advances. It finally came to blows [not physical] this particular night, and I remember thinking, *I have no choice but to tell him about what had happened to me as a girl.* I had been so afraid to reveal my secret to him for fear that he would think so much less of me, or worse, leave me. I remember saying to him "I have something to tell you." He listened as I tearfully told him every detail I could remember and just held me and cried with me, all the time telling me, "I'm so sorry this happened to you, sweetie."...So, two young kids expecting their first child, in a fairly new marriage, are left to pick up the pieces of this mess. Bruce was continually gracious with me and very self-sacrificing when it came to our intimacy. He never made me feel pressured or guilty for not having sex with him, yet I could see it taking its toll on my young husband.

After telling Bruce, Carrie decided she also wanted to tell her mother. The man who had abused Carrie almost married her mother. The abuse took place during her mother's involvement with this man. Bruce and Carrie agreed to first tell her mother's current husband, who had truly become Carrie's "Dad." They had rightly assessed that her mother would need support after hearing the story. Her mother felt such guilt about her own lack of awareness of what had happened to Carrie that she did not talk about it again with Carrie for a number of years.

The horrible memories of her experience continued to haunt Carrie. Their family grew and their relationship remained strong even though her experience of abuse had lasting effects on their intimacy. She prayed for God to "delete" her awful memories. Finally, through an experience with a ministry designed to help abuse survivors, Carrie was able to move toward more complete healing and final freedom from her secret experience.

We see here a healthy outcome from the painful and threatening telling of a shameful secret. The outcome could have been quite different. What if Carrie had continued to hold her secret and turned Bruce aside and never explained her past? Many marriages fail at this point when a shameful secret is not shared or when it is and the spouse cannot accept this news about the person they married. Perhaps realizing what some people carry into marriage could inform ministers to encourage couples to be open about secrets they bring to the marriage relationship. It is hard to imagine how many marriages might be saved by openness to telling and hearing shameful secrets.

Causing Others to Lie

We force some people into hiding when we demonstrate judgment and disapproval of, for example, out-of-marriage pregnancies or when we do not affirm choices mothers might make to relinquish their children for adoption. We push these mothers to live lives denying they ever gave birth to the child and judge them when they failed to try raising a child they did not feel they could raise. Entire lives become denial of the truth. We cannot ignore the amount of energy it takes to live lives in hiding to avoid judgment from others.

I am concerned about the pain and division that not telling the truth causes within families and communities. Families, in which there are members who are, for example, gay or incarcerated or who have AIDS, sometimes hide the existence of these family members, fearing the family will be judged and rejected. Some women who experience abuse from their husbands remain silent because they fear not only further abuse by their husbands but also being judged by their friends at church. Recall the women in Pastor Dan's church. Some couples live with great alienation in their relationship, but are forced by church and community attitudes to be deceptive about their situations. Community demands deception about what it does not want to know.

Part IV: Is What You Hear the Truth?

When someone confides a secret, this question about whether what you hear is the truth is realistic. We know that lies play a major role in keeping secrets. The dynamics between secret keeping and lying are complex because deception protects the secret keeper. Asking this question about the truth of what we are told invites us to *judge* what we hear. It also presumes that we can discern what is true and what is not true. Too often we choose to discern rather than receive. What we might better do is to welcome what is confessed with as little judgment as possible.

Secrets are sometimes outrageous and unbelievable in themselves. When we take into account how the secrets we hear may not fit with how we know the person who confesses the secret, this reality itself makes believing difficult. In addition, when the secret told involves someone else we know, our belief may be deeply challenged. A lot works against our trusting what we hear. Deception has served the secret keeper well, in keeping their shame safely hidden and, thus, keeping the secret holder safe. We can expect that what the speaker confesses has been embedded in deception.

When the secret holder has decided to tell what is shameful, perhaps hidden for a long time, that decision itself should support our trust in what is at the heart of the told secret. Knowing how difficult it is to decide to reveal what has been hidden contributes to our belief in its truth when we hear it. But discernment is vital when listening because some people are malicious and the secret they tell may be fabricated and meant to harm someone else, perhaps you. We should hold this suspicion but avoid rejection of the secret teller and seek to discern the truth in what is told.

Conclusion

We keep secrets and tell lies so that we won't get hurt; so others won't get hurt; so our lives can continue, our families remain intact, our communities still embrace us; so we can still belong and survive.

Secret keeping relies on deception. Therefore, we have compelling reasons to deceive.

Keeping secrets is not entirely wrong. We see how secrets and lies divert people (sometimes even the secret keeper) from the truth. We recognize that it may be a secret or a truth that cannot be faced or borne. It may be that the truth of a secret would harm others if it were spoken or revealed. This was a risk Carrie took in telling her husband and her mother.

Silence related to kept secrets may rob other people of information they need, while it robs the secret keeper of peace and wholeness in life. Understanding lying and deception and some of their causes helps us understand secrets and their keeping. Just like the truth being context appropriate, telling secrets is also context appropriate. Sometimes it is inappropriate to tell a secret because of the situation and others involved. Telling may be inappropriate when it would cause harm to others.

We have seen in this chapter how lies function in keeping secrets. We also recognize that secrets function out of a need to protect ourselves and others from both perceived and real manifestations of danger. In the next chapter, we will look at shame and how it functions in keeping secrets.

Chapter 5

Can Shame Release the Truth?

Introduction

Every secret with which this book is concerned is a secret filled with shame. Shame keeps secrets hidden. Even though the term *shame* is commonly used, our understanding of what it means may not be clear. Many times we use the terms *shame* and *guilt* interchangeably. Both shame and guilt are involved in kept secrets.

This chapter begins with a discussion of the meaning of shame and its role in human life and relationships. I will draw a distinction between shame and guilt in order to show how they play different roles in our lives. In relation to shameful secrets, the silence about the secret works to conceal the shame that would be exposed if anyone knew the secret. Although the keeper of the secret already feels shame, the threat of and possible exposure of the shame secure the *power* of the secret.

The idea is not to get rid of all shame, but to live with a healthy measure of shame. This chapter examines the healthy function of shame in our lives and helps readers distinguish between shame that helps us and shame that hinders us; minor shame and shame that hurts us. The chapter concludes with some directions for dealing with our shame.

The question with which we begin is whether the power of shame can allow us to release the truth.

Part I: Shame in Our Lives

Shame and Guilt

Shame is characterized by several words that suggest the involvement of loss—discredited, disgraced, dishonored—loss of credibility, loss of grace, loss of honor, and also, perhaps most important, loss of control. To be ashamed means we have lost these valuable and affirming aspects of being human. Shame implies feelings of humiliation and embarrassment and is caused by acts contrary to morality and modesty.

The existence of shame relies on a standard that is seen as generally accepted and enforced. If I do not live up to that standard, I feel shame. I feel others are looking down on me. Or I feel small, inadequate. Shame is caused by acts that are contrary to accepted morality and modesty. Beyond morality and modesty, shame emerges when we fall short of expectations we hold particularly for ourselves. Shame diminishes self-worth and distorts human life.

Shame *addresses us at the level of who we are* and *not just something we have done*. Here is its distinction from guilt. We feel guilt about particular acts we commit, or what we fail to do, behavior that is considered wrong. Guilt deals in specifics. But when we experience shame, we experience "wrongness" about our whole selves, our whole being. With shame I have not just *done* something wrong, but *I* am wrong. Shame is a total feeling about myself, whereas guilt limits itself to particular acts that I have done or should have done, witnessed, or in which I have participated.

Shame and guilt are distinct in the ways they are held. For example, when we have confessed something for which we feel guilt, we are more likely to be able to move on and no longer carry the guilt. With shame, confession offers a beginning of healing. There is still work to be done to deal with the depth and expanse of the shame.

Shame in Our Closest Relationships

Shame does not come upon us solely due to acts we have committed, but we are also ashamed of others related to us. Family members, most often, are ones who cause us shame. We experience shame because of what family members have done, what they look like, how they act, when they have failed, who they are, illnesses they have, or who they have become. Still, shame in these instances, becomes shame about *myself.* For example, I feel shame about being related to this other person, or I believe that somehow their behavior is a result of what I might have done wrong. The person's behavior or their being has brought shame on me and, as I see it, on our family, community, or even nation.

In some cultures when a family member brings shame on the family, the family response is to disown the offender, casting them out of the family, eliminating them from inheritance, even killing the offensive family member. The impact of shameful feelings is considerable across cultures and deeply rooted in cultural and faith expectations. A child grows up and informs his parents that he is gay. He may have put this announcement off for a long time because of fear of rejection by his parents. Parents feel shame about how others will look at them and the possibility that others might blame them for their child's sexual orientation. The parents know others are thinking, "He is that way because of something they have done." They are ashamed. They may take steps to distance themselves from their child in hope that the shame will not implicate them or that by rejecting their child, they will be redeemed in the eyes of others.

Part II: The Role Shame Plays in Our Lives

Growing Up with Shame

Unacceptable behavior of young children is sometimes met with the adult response, "Shame on you!" The child's response may include downcast eyes, covered face or eyes, bowed head, slumped shoulders, and the wish to disappear. "Shame on you," cuts to the soul. When being shamed becomes a common occurrence in a child's life, its impact diminishes the child's sense of self-esteem. The child's view of her or himself can become decidedly negative.

Adult reaction to feeling ashamed or being shamed remains hauntingly similar to the childhood response. Being made to feel ashamed creates a feeling of being diminished, reminding us of our childhood when we were little and had less power. We recognize limitations in our being able to assess what is appropriate. When we do know what is appropriate, we realize that we have lacked the ability to act according to accepted standards and expectations.

We do not have to be repeatedly, intentionally shamed to grow up with multiple feelings of shame. We accumulate many shameful views of ourselves through our perception of and acceptance of standards and judgments promoted by religion and by the society around us. We feel ashamed about who we are, what we do, and what we do not do. Only those possessing the ideals of economic wealth, youth, beauty, and positions with status and power—those of the "correct" race, gender, sexual orientation, and culture—are freed from the shame that prevails. Or so we think.

Religion plays a powerful role in creating shame when it centers its message on pronouncing judgment and promoting shame among its followers. The media promote shame in conveying to us who we ought to be and what we should own, what we should drive, and where we should shop and live.

Women, in particular, are encouraged to be ashamed of our bodies. The economic value of how we are encouraged to view ourselves is interesting. Notice the great numbers of products available to help women not be ashamed of their appearance. This assault only increases with aging. With the ever-present ideal image of youth in the media, we become ashamed of getting older, even before we are old. The natural process of aging (done differently by each person) is seen as a source of shame to be avoided at all cost.

Surrounded by images of abundance and extravagance, those of us who live below the poverty level or who receive general assistance are shamed. Those of us with disabilities are shamed by a society that values bodies and abilities. Those who have certain illnesses have been taught to feel shame about what is "wrong" with them or how they got sick. Despite the barrage of cultural or family messages we receive, some people are able to overcome imposed feelings of shame. When people do this in spite of how their circumstances may require shameful feelings, we are surprised. Shame is to be expected.

There is plenty of shame to go around, even before we begin to consider shameful secrets about traumatic experiences. The impact of the shame we experience around our kept secrets has life-shaping power.

Shamelessness

The other side of this overabundance of shame is shamelessness. A person who is shameless necessarily puts himself or herself or is put outside society. A person who behaves shamelessly is acting contrary to the accepted norms and values of their community and often in defiance. And anyone who feels *no* shame is not "socialized" into human community. In our society, we consider such behavior as antisocial, pathological, or criminal. We have to be able to feel shame in order to be a part of society. Human dignity, to some extent, depends on the function of shame. Shame keeps us from doing the unacceptable, what is considered as inappropriate in the society around us. We know that behaving in certain ways brings embarrassment on us. We also realize that we can do some things that are guaranteed to embarrass others.

We are socialized to avoid feeling ashamed. We do not want to be shamed. But with an absence of shame, what would life in society be like? When we watch certain kinds of television talk shows, we find an answer. There we can see folks who function with an apparent absence of shame. Participants demonstrate a lack of modesty or sense of what is appropriate. They perform in public, on television, in very extreme and exposed ways—in dress, behavior, and verbal expression. The audience as well behaves with little shame as they shout at, judge, and belittle those who are on stage.

Why are they *not* ashamed? Some of us who are watching feel shame for them. What keeps them from feeling ashamed? Some people claim that this lack of shame in public is an indication of the decline of civility and of society in general. I wonder if we have always had these obviously shameless folks with us, and now we just get greater exposure to them because there are so many opportunities for public exposure.

A Measure of Shame

Folks on these television shows, for example, seem to demonstrate a diminished capacity for shame; however, the degree of shame anyone feels may be based on many factors. Shame about a simple social faux pas does not usually shape our lives, but this kind of minor experience of shame remains with us, and we may be perfectly willing to tell the story of our shameful experience, even willing to feel minor embarrassment when the memory recurs.

Sparing Another from Shame

Connections between people lead us to an interesting dynamic regarding shame, because at times we make great efforts to assure that another person does not experience shame. We seek to spare them from shame. This is a crucial part of human civility. During the year after I completed my college education, I taught fifth grade in a public school in Indiana where I experienced an outstanding exhibition of this quality of human civility with those fifth graders.

At that time, there was no provision for special education for students who needed it. In the class was a boy I will call "Joey." Joey was unable to read or write. He was severely mentally challenged, but the school had chosen to move him along so that he could stay with kids his own age. I observed the children on the playground helping him participate in games; he was always included. Even so, I was totally unprepared for what happened in the classroom.

One day we were having a contest that involved students taking turns doing simple math problems in their heads. Joey's turn came and I asked him a very simple math problem. The answer he gave was incorrect. After only a brief pause, the best math student in the class, Wally, shouted, "Joey got it right! He got it right!" After a shocked moment of silence in the classroom, a moment of confused glances at one another, and particularly, at Wally, the other students joined in cheering for Joey. For only a moment, I considered my teaching role. Maybe I should assert that Joey's answer was not correct. Instead, I decided that the moment was more important than the math.

These students, together, demonstrated the reality that we can change a social response to include someone who is typically shamed. Their proclamation that Joey had "gotten it right" was an example of sparing human dignity for one who had so little opportunity to get his share. The students had rescued Joey from one moment of shame. Joey was beaming. I was dumbfounded by the generosity of spirit among these children who were, themselves, many times victims of shame, having been openly labeled in the school as "the slow class."

This experience is a startling contrast to the many times when those who are themselves ashamed feel compelled to shame others so that their own shame does not stand alone. Unfortunately, we see this too often around us and among us. This defensive shaming may be most obvious among children, but clearly it is not limited to them. Just take a glance back at the television talk shows in which the shaming of others slams back and forth between the guests and from guest to audience and back again. Even in the bravado often shown, the pain that shame creates is evident.

Shame and Privacy

The concept of privacy is important to any discussion of shame. What is done or said in private may be quite appropriate when in private, but very inappropriate in public. What is shared with intimate friends or with family may be appropriate there in relative privacy, or with a select audience, or a counselor or pastor, but not in public.

When a stranger or casual acquaintance shares intimate details of his or her life, this sharing may be a violation of both the privacy the person should maintain and a violation of the person who is told. "Too much information" is a felt response of the listener under such circumstances. "Keep it to yourself. This is not information that anyone who is not close to you (or not paid to hear it) wants to hear." Listeners seek to protect themselves from an assault of information or behavior that is felt as inappropriate. We feel we have the right not to have such personal exposure foisted upon us. Shame can function to protect us from unwanted, inappropriate exposure.

Shame always has to do with being caught, discovered, and exposed. Many common nightmares include scenes in which we are facing shame—being in front of a group without clothes on, being unprepared for an exam, being exposed and being vulnerable. Experiencing these dreams, we remind ourselves of feelings of shame.

Shame for What Another Has Done

When a person has been the victim of abuse perpetrated by another person, the victim feels shame about what has been done to them. What has been done in violence and violation causes victimized persons to experience themselves in a shameful way. Thus, keepers of secrets who have been abused or violated by others feel shame about their experience even though they did not cause the experience. When we are not at fault, we can still find ways to blame ourselves for what has been done to us. Telling what has happened, we fear, will confirm our role and solidify that shame.

A common shame experience for families occurs when a family member commits suicide. It is extremely difficult for a family to avoid feeling shame about a suicide. It does not matter which member of the family it is. There is always guilt because of suspicions that "we could/

should have done something" to prevent it. There is something about our family that is wrong and caused the suicide. We are ashamed that someone in our family could have committed suicide. When possible, many families keep this cause of death secret. The pain and the shame often linger in the family for generations. Harold Ivan Smith, in his book about suicide, *A Long Shadowed Grief,* reveals to his readers the suicide secrets of many prominent families, and how these secrets have been passed from one generation to the next, remaining hidden to the public if not in the family.[1]

Shame also exists in relation to secrets kept about what a person has witnessed. Often the witnessed event was perpetrated by a relative or another close person. The shame is still about *my self.* "Maybe I could have done something to stop what happened." Usually, this conclusion is neither logical nor reasonable, but it is a real feeling. Traumatic experience causes change in self-perception. Sometimes my identity becomes linked to the violence done, for example, I may experience my identity as "the one who witnessed my friend being raped." What is witnessed may be so unbelievable that even all our certainty about what we experienced may be doubted.

Part III: Shame in Balance

Shame in Human Development

Human development expert Erik Erikson presented an understanding of human growth in terms of life stages. Throughout life, at each stage, we are challenged to achieve a balance between two polar dynamics, referred to by Erikson as "Psychosocial Themes." He identifies the second stage of life as focused on a balance between autonomy on one hand and shame and doubt on the other.[2] Since we value autonomy and are uncomfortable with shame and doubt, an immediate response is to see autonomy as being positive and shame and doubt as being negative. In each of the stages that Erikson names, however, the goal is to develop a healthy balance between the two potential extremes.

Autonomy is a highly valued characteristic in much of American society. In this discussion we need to keep in mind that perspectives on shame and autonomy differ from one society to another. The differences are sometimes quite dramatic. What we discuss here is clearly from a predominantly American perspective. Both shame and autonomy are valued differently elsewhere. Autonomy means the ability to determine for oneself events in one's life. *Independence* is another word we generally use for it. Autonomy is positive. However, when we think about autonomy, taken to an extreme, that would mean the absence of any balance with shame and doubt. We begin to see the difficulty with being too autonomous. Acting with total autonomy from everyone else, absent of any shame or doubt, we function in society without regard for any others. In absolute autonomy there is no room for taking others into account. We function solely in our own interest. Taken to an extreme, autonomy can come at a high cost to self and others.

A Balance between Autonomy and Shame and Doubt

We might find it difficult to value shame in our lives when we look at its negative effect in the lives of so many people. But when we take a closer look, we are encouraged to think of stages in life as involving the resolution of a balance between what appear to be positive and negative poles. I find it helpful to think in terms of the following chart:

	Autonomy	Balance	Shame
Attitude	"I am self-sufficient."	"I am limited."	"I am defective."
Behavior	Disregard for others. Excessive regard for self.	Appropriate regard for self and others. "I am part of a community."	Disregard for self. Excessive regard for others.
Claim	"You need me. I don't need you."	"We need each other."	"I need you. You don't need me."

When I live at the extreme of autonomy, I live without regard for others. I am the only one who determines my destiny, and this is my sole concern. I do not need others. We all go through stages in life when we lean more heavily toward the extreme of autonomy. The "terrible twos" and teenage years are notable seasons for potentially excessive autonomy.

At the other extreme of the spectrum is a feeling of total disregard for oneself. It may be surprisingly easy to find pure examples of this extreme. However, I suspect that many of the people reading this book live on the median between "balance" and "shame." Some of us have the tendency to hold ourselves in less regard than we hold others. Religion sometimes supports our leaning toward this pole. Oddly, accepting the reality that, as human beings, we are limited, in both who we are and what we can do, seems to be more difficult for us to accept than is the other extreme of seeing ourselves as defective. There we remain, full of shame. However, as human beings we live in need of community. Without one another we cannot continue to exist as God's human creation.

Shame alienates us from others just as much as does a lack of shame. As part of a human community we live as people who are limited and accepting of our selves and of our need for others. This human community, where we stand in need of the others who stand with us, seeks to live in balance between autonomy and shame. In community we exist with others who are always different from ourselves. We live with these differences and learn to trust those different others and the gifts they bring in order to be a community. In reality, we do not exist without community. An African saying affirms, "I am because we are."[3] But within community I also need to find others who are like me in some ways, in order to be able to find my place. To live in community means it is necessary to rely on other limited human beings and, within that community, find that they also rely on me. At our best, together we share trust because we realize the mutuality essential in community.

Part IV: Shame in Our Secrets

Shame attached to experiences that are traumatic does not allow for the easy telling of our secrets. Here, the degree of shame is deep and painful. The shame my mother experienced regarding the abuse by her father was this kind of shame. We become silent. Relationships are limited. We keep parts of our selves hidden. We limit what we will do. Shame, to this extent, imprisons us in many ways, thereby having a lasting impact on our lives. We have a constant, present fear of being exposed as long as we keep shameful secrets. Along with fear of exposure, we anticipate certain rejection and isolation.

Living with Shame

There was a woman I will call Margaret, who took her secret and turned its burden into motivation to excel. Margaret shows us another path of shame.

Even though living a good life provides an effective screen to hide a secret, we discover that the secret has still been a burden. We meet her late in her life as she struggles with deciding whether to tell her secret to her family. Surprisingly, some people make positive choices in response to keeping shameful secrets.[4]

The Perfect Screen for Hiding Shameful Secrets

Margaret was a valued and faithful church member and leader (deacon and church school teacher), beloved wife, mother and grandmother, an active and respected contributor in the community. Margaret came to her pastor with a deep concern. It took Margaret some time to be able to say what was troubling her. She clearly harbored some fear about how the pastor would see her once he discovered what she was going to say. Finally, she revealed her secret.

When she was very young, still in college and single, Margaret had gotten pregnant and had an abortion. At that time she lived in another state. She had not yet met the man who would become her husband. There were no close family members around to discover her secret. Following college, she relocated to her current community, where no one knew her or her secret. Margaret literally started a whole new life.

From its inception, she carried her secret all alone. She finally felt an urgency to confess her secret. She overcame her internal resistance and misgivings in order to speak to her pastor. Somehow, she realized that her pastor was safe enough to trust with her secret.

After she told her secret, Margaret proceeded to ask her pastor how he felt about her. She entered into the conversation with fear that his view of her would be changed as soon as he heard her secret. She had to overcome this fear to be able to talk with him. Her pastor expressed no judgment toward Margaret or her secret. Instead, he expressed appreciation of her courage to tell him her secret. He was understanding and invited her to talk about how she made her decision to tell the secret after all this time.

The Need to Tell

Margaret told him she was feeling a need to tell her family the secret. No one knew. She had carried this burden alone, all of her adult life. She had never told her recently deceased husband and felt very guilty about that. She was aware of the approach of the end of her own life, a life that had been full of energy, integrity, and blessings. She was unable to see how to fit her past experience and kept secret into the same picture with the rest of her life. Margaret deeply felt the discrepancy between how she had led the rest of her life, and this single secret event from her past. She longed to resolve the disparity, in some way. Telling her secret was the only way she could see to resolve her dilemma.

Margaret came to her pastor to ask him whether she should tell someone in her family and also if she should tell people in the church. She was torn about whether to tell or not tell. She clearly feared that the respect she had earned over decades of good living would all be washed away with a confession about her past. Yet, she felt the need to tell, to (in her words) "wipe the slate clean." As things stood, she felt she was living a lie. Because of her secret "no one," she felt, "knew the *real Margaret*." She felt like a fraud.

She felt guilt about letting her husband die without telling him her secret. He died thinking she was someone who she knew she was not. She had been living a lie all of these years. All of this weighed heavily on Margaret. The pressing reality of her deception was compelling her to tell.

The issue of telling had begun to trouble Margaret as her husband had been dying, but she had so much to attend to during that time that she had kept the telling question on the back burner and had not come to a decision before his death. The fact of not having told her dear husband added to the burden she felt now of not being truthful with others in the family. After his death, she made a commitment to herself that she would make the decision whether to tell others or not. Making the commitment to decide somewhat eased her pain about not telling her husband. Her resolution to decide now brought Margaret into conversations with her pastor. Her pastor wisely knew not to answer Margaret's questions about telling. This was her work to do and her decision to make.

Resistance to Telling

Margaret took a shameful experience and kept it secret for more than fifty years. It required a lot of energy to hold the secret; to forever be concerned—although not always consciously—about someone discovering it. The secret also turned out, in her life, to be a motivator. Her life as known by the community, the church, and by her family had been outstanding. She was a living example to everyone of how to be a Christian and a good citizen.

As she spoke with the pastor, she identified her guilt and shame as playing a role in her efforts to be as good as she could be. She produced a lovely family, was a partner in an exemplary marriage, and gave much to both church and community. Her life was the very image of faithfulness and integrity. These were choices she made as her way to respond to the shame she felt. Her outstanding life had been, at least in part, constructed for the sake of remaining hidden. She reached for perfection in every aspect of her life. Margaret did not merely meet expectations but went beyond every expectation. Perfection was, for

Margaret, the ideal screen for hiding her secret. No one would question a life lived so perfectly. She was safe.

The pastor tried to help her weigh the benefits and the risks of telling her secret, leaving it to Margaret to decide whether, how, whom to tell, and when. They had numerous conversations about sorting through her decisions around her secret—to tell or not to tell. There was no one who suspected her secret, she was absolutely certain. She *could* keep her secret and, as many secret keepers say, "take it to my grave with me," and no one would be the wiser.

Her pastor turned out to be a very appropriate person with whom to discuss her concern, because there was a question for Margaret underneath this secret—a question about God's view of her. It was not, for her, a question of whether God *knew* about the secret, but a question of whether she still was loved by God. Her concern about how God saw her was particularly about her having deceived everyone all of these years—especially those closest to her. In addition, would her faith community accept her, if they knew *all* about her? If they wouldn't, had she any right to their acceptance of her as the person they *thought* her to be? Margaret had a big agenda.

As Margaret struggled with the decision to tell or not to tell, feeling pressure that she must let others know who she really was, she also feared the fallout from others finding out. She spent her life striving to be impeccable and succeeded. Now, if she told others the truth, her whole image would be shattered. The respect others had for her and their admiration could vanish. They would, of course, begin to wonder what else they did not know about her. Her identity in their eyes (which had never been congruent with her own self-image) could be destroyed. All of this played itself out as Margaret tried to decide whether she could tell the truth about her secret.

Since Margaret had climbed so high in others' estimations of her, she was clear that she had that much further to fall. It helped that the pastor did not react with rejection, disillusionment, or judgment toward Margaret. Still, she would need great courage to tell others, because she might stand to lose such a great deal.

Would Margaret have been able to trust her pastor to listen and continue to care about her, if he had preached sermons condemning abortion? This situation provides an illustration of how pastors can close doors to people who need to confess their secrets. Notice, too, that her concern about how God saw her was about her having deceived people for so many years. It was not about having had an abortion. If the pastor had not heard her and instead mistakenly assumed what was troubling in her relationship with God, he would have missed her true concern.

Margaret's Response to Feeling Shame

Living above reproach, as Margaret did, enables secret keepers to throw others off the track of discovering their shameful secrets. It is a cover that defies suspicion. People do not tend to question what appears to be a perfect life. No one suspects there is something hidden. Perfection is a cover that also keeps the secret keeper very busy. Uneasiness existed throughout her whole life, in spite of the way Margaret turned her shame and secret into achievement. Margaret's dedication to excellence kept her conscious mind off of her secret and allowed her to focus on her efforts to succeed—Margaret's way of hiding. We can see both—Margaret's focus on keeping the secret, which demands her attention, *and* her being busy with success that keeps her *from* focusing on her secret.

Margaret, of course, does not stand alone as someone who responded to a shameful secret in a way that brings the best out of their lives. Other people discover that their kept secrets drive them in positive directions. People find occupations and commitments that emerge out of their own kept secrets, or the secrets that shaped their lives, through their parents' or families' secrets. Such a direction should not be disparaged. People do positive things out of negative motivators, and the positive things they do are still positive, regardless of what may be seen as their negative origins. Positive outcomes can be events of grace, even when they may have had negative origins.

We might wonder what Margaret would have been able to accomplish if she had not given so much of her life energy and attention to keeping her secret. This is all hypothetical, but I see two possibilities for Margaret. First, without her secret, she may have chosen to live a rather ordinary, unexceptional life. Another alternative for Margaret-without-a-secret might have been that she would have achieved *even more* than she was able to with the secret pushing her to achieve. Without the secret, she could have used her *whole* self. We cannot determine which possibility would have occurred, because we do not get to see Margaret, with all of her gifts and energy, live out her life without her secret, nor is it possible to make a direct comparison between Margaret and any other person.

Autonomy or Shame for Margaret

At first glance, we see Margaret as someone who appears to be living near the balance between autonomy and shame. She obviously demonstrates regard for others and functions as one who recognizes that she is a part of, and a contributor to, a community. It appears to others that Margaret also has regard for herself. We see her as one who established and maintained what appear to be healthy relationships with others, within the family and beyond the family. All of this looks like a person living in "balance territory." But what about the shame we discovered, which has been her lifelong companion?

Margaret managed to live as though she was a person without shame, while she was a person driven by shame. We saw in her story the depth of shame that demanded that she carry her secret for her whole adult life, that prevented her from being able to tell her ailing husband about her past, and that now keeps her from deciding to tell others for whom she cares deeply. We heard her feelings about herself, which sounded like she sees herself as defective—otherwise wouldn't she think others would still accept her, if they knew her secret?

We see Margaret's behavior as balanced, but what we learn about her shows us a discrepancy. Internally, Margaret lives much closer to shame than to balance. Margaret's relationships appear to be healthy, but we do not know about their mutuality. Is Margaret able to receive from others as well as she can give to others?

Another question remains as we think about Margaret telling her secret. If she was able to perform so effectively, carrying her shameful secret (and with what we suspect is a significant level of low self-esteem at the same time), what will happen to her level of self-esteem when she reveals her secret? She expects that others' esteem of her will be reduced. Once the secret is out will Margaret begin to see *herself* in a whole new light? This will depend, in part, on how others react to hearing her secret. If they are accepting of her *with her secret,* as the pastor was, then maybe she will be able to be more accepting of herself. Could her pastor's acceptance, love, and grace be misleading and the people of the congregation be not so accepting and grace-filled? Even if people are affirming and accepting after hearing her secret, will Margaret be able to believe this is true? Has she built such expectation of rejection and judgment that she would not even receive their acceptance?

We leave Margaret here without knowing the conclusion of her story. We do not know what she decided to do about telling others. We do not know whether others were accepting and understanding, if she told her secret. However, not knowing the outcome does not make Margaret's story any less valuable to our understandings about how shame functions in secret keepers' lives.

The Barriers to Telling

As we see with Margaret, sometimes people overcome huge barriers in order to tell their secrets. Lack of a place where one could speak is one barrier for many secret keepers. For my mother there was no forum in which her secret could be spoken and heard. During her youth and childhood, incest was never mentioned and sex was not discussed. She carried the shame without community to sustain her or support her. Fearing isolation and rejection if she told, she had to bear her secret in isolation.

My mother was compelled not to tell her secret throughout her life, even though she realized as a child the wrongness of what her father did to her. She was clearly ashamed of *herself.* She lived her life somewhere in between balance and shame. Her attitude toward life was that *she* was defective. She consistently demonstrated more regard for others than for herself. She felt her need for others and did not experience their need for her. She lived her life with shame, as she kept the secret of her abuse.

Moving from Shame

Shame is sustained by isolation and shattered by community. Nowhere is this more obvious than in the communities of Twelve Step programs. In Alcoholics Anonymous the tradition is to introduce one's self, "Hello, my name is Robert, and I'm an alcoholic." Those gathered respond, "Hello, Robert." In this response, it is clear that the people present will hear and receive Robert. This organization knows something essential about what needs to happen to overcome shameful secrets.

With this formalized greeting and response, Robert immediately becomes part of a group in which everyone shares similar secrets. People do not move forward and come to healing if they deny that they are alcoholics. Denial hasn't worked, doesn't work, and will never work. In order to stop the denial and expose the secret, it is necessary to affirm honestly and openly, "My name is Robert, and *I am* an alcoholic." This exposure is not done in isolation. Others who are on the same road occupy the room. They make similar confessions.

In Alcoholics Anonymous, those who are ready to do so tell their stories. Robert goes on to present all of the shameful things he has done in vivid detail: losing family and job, being found on the sidewalk covered in vomit, "blacking out," squandering all of his money on drink—the lying, the hiding. All of these experiences are shameful, and now Robert confesses them before a group of people as his story. Defying previous fear of discovery, this alcoholic reveals everything.

When people stand and introduce themselves, they join a company of others who are in the same boat. Telling the story breaks the isolation of denial and secret keeping, and while some continue to drink and experience the shame related to it, others find they have begun to break free from the shame and cannot continue living the secret. Revealing one's secret acts as an affirmation of one's self. The words say, "This is who I am. This is what I have done." Shame has been surrounding that identity, and now Robert owns his life and it can, within this community, be transformed.

The new road taken is now the road to recovery and healing. Robert begins to break the control that shame had on his life. He begins to overcome the power shame holds on him. The community lends him strength. Community support works, as others are willing to be there when he needs someone for support to continue his healing. Each Twelve-Step member has a sponsor on whom they can rely for twenty-four hour availability when they feel vulnerable. The community goes beyond hearing the first confession and travels the road with Robert toward healing. Robert will probably tell his story over and over in his process of recovery.

A Model for Meeting Shame

In the introduction ritual of A. A., we find a model of what we need for healing from shameful secrets. The context is a *community ready to receive the secret* and offer support. Support is available both before and after the secret is exposed. People present have similar secrets that they too reveal. Robert anticipated neither judgment nor rejection. Instead he discovers their willingness to listen and *continue in relationship*. This experience of confession and community neutralizes the shameful fears of the secret keeper.

Conclusion

We begin to experience shame as children and live surrounded by shame in society. It is important that we not see shame as totally negative because living shameless also creates unhealthy communities. Leaders working in total autonomy are most likely to contribute to this unhealthiness. We realize that not all shame is of the same intensity. We see that important distinctions should be made between shameful hiding and maintaining personal or family privacy.

In previous chapters we looked at those who may be seen as wounded and limited people. We may feel sadness at the losses they have experienced as the result of difficult secrets that have caused them shame. What we have also seen here is an example of those secret keepers who accomplish remarkable things. Out of their pain they continue to struggle through life and become significant contributors to society. We would do them a great injustice to see them as incomplete, wounded, and never healed. This is, in part, certainly true, but it is not the whole picture. It is not all there is to them. It is also inappropriate to see them as people who stand in no need for healing, because we have seen the degree of shame the kept secret can embody for the keeper.

People are able to overcome shame and speak about their kept secrets when there is an open community willing and able to receive the person's story and to walk with them toward healing. The kind of affirmative community that needs to be present for the telling of shameful secrets may be found in places of faith or places like Alcoholics Anonymous and other Twelve-Step programs where people can experience affirmation in spite of their story. Shame can feel so overwhelming, and the telling of secrets can seem so threatening; it is no wonder it is so difficult for people to expose shameful secrets they carry.

Chapter 6

How Memory Helps, Defends, and Distorts

Introduction

How reliable is memory? When secrets have been kept for some time, can we trust that the memories are still reliable? In order to talk about secrets and their confession, we must consider memory. How memory functions and how trustworthy memory is are both concerns we encounter when we face secrets.[1] Memory holds secrets, sometimes from others and sometimes even from the one who has the secret. Yet, we rely on memory to give us the possibility for releasing secrets. Without an understanding of memory we don't know whether or how to trust the truth of our memories—the truth of our own secrets or secrets told to us.

Memory functions in ways that help, defend, and distort. These three functions are not easily separated. For example, memory distortions can both defend us and help us. Memories defending us may do so by using distortion. Even though we might immediately see distortions as negative, with further exploration we may discover how distortions help us. We cannot judge remembering as only positive and forgetting as only negative. Remembering can be a problem and forgetting a blessing.

Theologically, memory finds a central place in both Jewish and Christian faiths and faith practices.[2] Faith is rooted in memory. Every act of communion in churches is a ritual of remembering. The memory of the redeeming sacrifice of Jesus Christ is the heart of what Christians believe and profess. We recognize in our faiths how much of what we remember relies on those who went before us. The Jewish faith is rooted in remembering that Jews were once slaves in Egypt, a memory affirming that God rescued them as a people from Egypt. Our memories hold us in our faiths and bind our faith communities together. Memory defines our faith identities.[3]

Part I: The Roles of Memory

Shaping Identity

In part, at least, we *are* our memories. Memories make us who we are, participating in making us individuals. Memory plays an indispensable role in shaping our identities. Who I understand myself to be is constructed from a network of what I remember from my past experiences.[4] I also recognize that memories others have of me participate in my understanding of who I am. Memory not only tells us about our past, it informs our present and helps us move into our future. We all carry collections of both negative and positive memories of our own, in addition to memories we inherit from family stories. We study history and engage in communities where we also receive stories that we hold as memories.

With reflection I see how seemingly small pieces of my past have played roles in shaping the person I have become, and I can see how they continue to participate in who I will become. I recall pieces of my past experiences that I wish were not part of my past or part of my memories; rough times in life, joys, failures, mistakes, good and bad choices, losses, and hurts, both given and received. But they are all there, the good and the bad and the neutral. I realize how the bad has been part of shaping who I have become and will become. I realize that keeping some of these pieces means I carry painful memories. However, when the pain is too great, my memory may help me keep such memories hidden.

Of course, my memories are not limited to negative experiences. They include many incidents that carry joy and delight, and these memories also play a role in who we become and how we imagine our future. We inherit a legacy of memories from those who went before us. These memories play roles in shaping our identities. They enable us to imagine futures in which we meet struggles with strength and endurance, contrary to negative memories that we carry alongside the positive. Some memories that lead us to imagining a positive future involve struggles faced and troubles endured. These originally negative memories become gifts we inherit in which we can celebrate and anticipate our future overcoming.

Enabling Us to Function

We use memory to fulfill obligations, perform tasks, and relate to others. We maintain a store of memories, not necessarily all conscious, that enables us to perform even the simplest of tasks. Without memory from one day to the next, we are unable to maintain relationships, to carry out work, to be participants in families and communities. Our memories clearly enable us to function in every dimension of our everyday lives.[5]

Very young children are able to report memories they have that are unique to them. When they share memories of experiences shared with their parents, it becomes clear that they shaped their own memories. Their individualized memory is one way they develop separate identities.

Persons who experience dementia, either themselves or through the life of a loved one, recognize the considerable role memory plays in identity, in day-to-day life, and in relating. Loved ones experience the person with increasing dementia as "slipping away from them." Finally, they express their feeling that the loved one is "gone." The recognition of the use of memory comes by the power of its decline and, finally, its absence. With no memory we don't grow, we cannot learn, and we increasingly lose our selves.

The movie *Memento* demonstrates how difficult it is to live without memory. The central character in the story, Leonard, has lost his ability to form new memories due to a violent brain injury. He knows who he was before the injury, but not who he is now. We see his struggle with trying to function in the world. He tells us, "Memories are just an interpretation. Memory can change the shape of a room. It can change the color of a car. Memories can be distorted. They're just an interpretation, not a record. They're irrelevant, if you have the facts." Leonard expresses the struggles with which we are dealing. He recognizes that memories are questionable and involve interpretation. He realizes that memory and facts may not agree. Leonard is caught between trying to get and keep the facts and his memory's failure to give him assistance in the process. We see him become frantic trying to find a pen when he needs to write something down before he "loses" it. He knows his experience will be gone from his mental reach within seconds.

Leonard devised a way to manage his life by taking Polaroid photos of his car, where he lives, and the people he meets. He makes notes on the photos as reminders to help him recognize their significance. The notes tell him what he has learned about a person of whom he has taken a photograph. Sometimes he is forced to correct previous notes he has made when he obtains information contradictory to his previous experiences.

The desk clerk at the motel where he is living tries to take advantage of Leonard's condition. When Leonard has forgotten his room key, the clerk confesses to Leonard that, at the prompting of his boss, he has rented two rooms to Leonard, because he "wouldn't remember anyway." We do not fully appreciate that at every moment we rely on memory. Without it we are at the mercy of others.

Leonard must make memos to himself, clearly and thoroughly, or he is literally lost. He has especially important notes to himself tattooed on parts of his body because he must not get mixed up about the most important things. When Leonard pulls back his sleeve and sees a note on his arm, it seems to the viewer that the tattoo comes as a complete surprise to him. Of course it would be surprising. He didn't remember it! The memos and tattoos are his only way to remember his current life. He also uses memos to remind himself to do everyday functions such as shaving.

Those viewing this movie have a vicarious experience of not having memory because we can experience through Leonard what it can mean not to remember. The audience is disoriented because events in the movie are not presented in chronological order. The viewer does not have a memory of what has happened on which to rely. Throughout the movie it is clear that Leonard feels very unsafe and vulnerable. Since he cannot trust his memory, he cannot trust anyone or anything else. It is a troubling and painful movie. Leonard remembers no one in his current life.

Normal circumstances are more like this: I am a person who grew up in Cincinnati with two parents, a brother, and numerous animals. My memories further distinguish who I am as I recall relatives, friendships from childhood, my first job at a drug store soda fountain, the classes I enjoyed at school, and playing in the school band. All of these pieces have created who I know myself to be. They not only remain as little pieces that contribute to how I see myself but also function to inform what I do today—how I function under different circumstances that become related in some way to my past.

Even though I no longer live in Cincinnati, my parents and brother are no longer living, I have lost touch with many early friends, I have quite a different job, and I no longer play the drums, all of these pieces from long ago remain significant parts of my past and my present. These remembered pieces of my life remain a part of me. They are with me in the present and they contribute to my future. Memories participate in creating me as I move through life.[6]

Enabling Relationships

Without memories of my past and memories of recent experiences, I do not have an identity. Life does not make sense to me. Relationships do not evolve and cannot be sustained according to community standards. Continuity in life tells me both who I am and where I am going, even if it is just to the grocery store. Memory is significant in every part of our lives.

Memory tells me when a person I meet is someone I know, and, when it is someone I know, memory tells me the nature of our relationship. Leonard from *Memento* demonstrated a way to replace this memory function with the memos he wrote to himself on the Polaroid pictures he took of acquaintances. While it seems that we cannot be ourselves without memory, there are significant parts of being human that may continue to be "particularly us" even when we do not remember. Do we remain in these ways "ourselves," even without our memories? I am doubtful. Alzheimer's provides experiences of troubling change when someone we have known is no longer the person we had known them to be.

Memory and Forgetting

In spite of the significant role memory plays, it is a common human experience to feel a troubling lack of control over memory. We don't really have to get to middle age before we are telling ourselves that lapses in memory are age related. I know that age isn't completely to blame for memory lapses because I have lived with children. My sons, throughout all of their childhood years, were often not able to remember where they left their shoes just moments earlier.

Author Jean Beaven Abernethy provides an interesting perspective on experiencing memory lapses. "Most of us think forgetting goes with old age." She reflected that *everyone* forgets, but when we get old *we remember that we forget.*[7]

Much is lost to memory because we cannot keep in memory everything that passes through our lives.[8] Take a moment and think about what it would mean to consciously remember *everything*. Events in lives hold different degrees of meaning for those who experience them. Some things are of minor importance in the grand scheme of things.

Strangely, some of such minor experiences do become permanent in our memories without apparent reason.

A great deal of what I have experienced in my life *seems* to be lost to my memory. This does not mean that I have made an effort to repress or forget these lost pieces, but that I experience that they seem to have slipped away. A friend will say, "Remember when . . . ?" and I will draw a complete blank. I don't have a clue about what they are trying to remind me. It works the other way around, too. I will say, "Remember when . . . ?" and I will receive the blank look. In the case of a memory I cherish, I want to precede my question with, "Please say that you remember. I want to be right about this memory because it is important to me."

Several years ago I was reunited with my best friend from childhood, Lucille. I traveled back to my hometown for the occasion of her mother's birthday. We discovered with pleasant surprise that we still held the same memory of a little song we had created so many years earlier, in elementary school. I felt, surely she couldn't have remembered this ridiculous thing. Indeed, she did, and we sang it together once more—same tune, same words. There is no way to see a purpose for remembering something like this other than to remind us of who we are and who we are together.

Human beings have developed an ability to keep information we need and jettison what we do not need. In the process of choosing what they should preserve, our memories may make (what we experience as) errors or mistakes and "throw out" memories we may actually come to need. On the other hand, we are kept safe by our memory with its ability to forget that *with which we cannot live.*[9] Forgetting is an action of the subconscious in these cases and not a mistake.

Experts in remembering and courses that teach memory skills demonstrate that we can remember far more than we usually remember or think we *can* remember.[10] Training oneself to remember can be very effective. We recognize with amazement the degree to which some people have trained their memories and those who are simply gifted with the ability to remember much more than the average person. We put this ability to remember at varying levels alongside the reality of memory limitations experienced so commonly and see a diverse picture of memory.

We also forget what we are told to forget. Abusers of all sorts tell their victims to forget what has happened, sometimes with a threat attached. These orders lead to what has been called *repressed memories*. Adult relatives tell children to forget events that they do not want kept as part of the family history and which they certainly do not want shared outside of the family. The society around us also tells us to forget some things. For example, forget aspirations that are not realistic for you because of your gender, your age, your economic status, your racial or ethnic heritage, or your family's class.

Memories of traumatic events that we are told to forget do, however, tend to remain with us even when we do not remember that we keep them.[11] Some things we do not have to be told to forget in order to know that we are supposed to forget. Adults may presume that children are too young to remember some traumatic event and act like the event didn't happen, so the message for the child involved is an unspoken "do not remember." A child may share a memory with an adult and the adult will tell them it didn't happen. We readily learn when things are to be kept secret. We learn from our own feelings of shame that seep in around experiences, informing our feelings and actions following the experience. Keeping memories secret from others and from ourselves sometimes serves the urgent purpose of keeping us safe—protecting our selves and our relationships.

Memories Made to Fit

We forget or distort memories that do not fit with a predominant view of how we see ourselves. Individuals, families, communities, and nations function with these distortions of memory. For example, we may glorify Native Americans and their culture and fail to remember the long and deadly Trail of Tears many were forced to walk toward their relocation in areas designated by colonizing powers. We not only forget, we also replace what truly took place with invented "histories" of things that were not true events. Individually and communally we revise histories. Sometimes on a more individual level *replacement memories* are constructed by our brains to provide stories that are more congruent with what we understand as our identity and self-image. This rewriting occurs by individuals, families, churches, and nations. We should be cautious about what is revised history, since it is sometimes done with a particular political agenda.

The replacement of memories that do not fit an image with memories that do fit also has to do with other people. We replace memories we have of experiences with others. We get our memories to fit *our image* of who *we* expect them to be, or who *we* are in relation to them. I remember my childhood and youth as including occasional mischief, disobedience, and recklessness. In her old age my mother always said I was a "perfect child," never any trouble. I think, "Oh, sure." Mother revised my early history to concur with her image of me as the good daughter.

Part II: Memory in Context

As we consider memory, it is important to take a brief look at some particular contexts in which memory functions. Reflection on the contexts of memory gives us another advantageous perspective on understanding memory.

The Context of Faith

Every faith is rooted in memory. Rituals function as acts of remembering. Remembering contributes to holding us together as a religious community. Confession, as a religious act, is itself an act of memory as it involves revealing what we remember as needing to be confessed according to our faith tradition. Memory holds expectations our faith has for our behavior. Memory makes faith possible, which is clearly one way in which it functions to heal and help us.

In the context of faith, we also discover that distortions in memory are common. We take images from scripture, for example, and interpret them in ways that make them agree with what we want to see or believe. They remain in our memories and are passed on in the way we see them. For example, we may be reluctant to see that Jesus actually learned something from the Syrophoenician woman when he refused her request to heal her daughter, which resulted in her challenging his claim that he came only for the people of Israel. She responded to his view of his ministry as being limited. She told him that even the dogs eat the crumbs under the table. Jesus affirmed that because of what she has said her daughter was healed. We want to see this event as Jesus testing the woman, perhaps because we cannot accept that Jesus actually learned something he didn't know or that he learned something from the woman (Mark 7:26-30). Many of us remember that this is how we should understand this story.

The Context of Community

Beyond the community context of religious bodies, memories create and bind all kinds of communities together. We are together because of memories we hold in common. Without shared memories we don't become or remain communities. The importance of memories for communities is demonstrated in the ways we memorialize important people, places, events, and things. War memorials remind us of lives lost and victories won. They also remind us of conflicts that remain not only remembered but also that are still very much alive among us.

I recall seeing a huge statue in a park in Dallas. The statue memorialized those who fought for the South in the Civil War. It didn't strike me as an ambiguous memorial when I first saw it. Then, while I was in South Africa, a friend showed me a prominent place where there had been a statue. The statue base was empty. The friend explained that the statue that had been there was one of a former South African president who had enforced apartheid. With the coming of the new post-apartheid government, the statue was removed to a government building. Its new location made it less prominent, offering a way to now honor the country's new direction. While the statue remained in the city center, it was a public and bold reminder of apartheid's oppression. In the Dallas park, the Civil War monument, still prominent, affirms a past that many of us believe should no longer be so obviously affirmed. Maybe it could be placed in a less conspicuous location like the statue in South Africa was, indicating less celebration of the South's fight for slavery.

What do we want to be reminded of by our memorials? They can be another function of memory distortions or denials as well as being reminders of victory over negative situations. There are memorials that have been slow to come to being or that have yet to appear. These may honor what we fail to value. Both the Vietnam Memorial and the memorial to Dr. Martin Luther King, Jr. were slow to materialize, but memorials always call us to remember. They call on our memories. Miraslov Volf encourages us to "remember rightly" and reminds us that memories are not a private matter.[12]

Spontaneous memorials spring up in places where someone died in an accident or where someone was killed. Statues of famous people remind us of their achievements and what they have meant to us as a people. Memorials remind us of events in our national history. The memorial of the bombing of the Oklahoma City government building is a striking example. Empty chairs, each bearing the name of a victim of the attack, overlook a pool located at the former site of the building. Visitors to Oklahoma City visit this site and remember what happened there and the lives that were lost. Memorials remind us and bind us together through the memories we share.

In addition to elaborate memorials and smaller spontaneous ones, we also celebrate Memorial Day—a day of remembering our veterans—and hold memorial services that identify the value to us, as communities, of remembering others. We remember anniversaries of important events and celebrate memories of those who have died.

The Context of Imagination

Imagination is tightly interwoven with memory. Imagination plays a role in what we see and how we interpret what we see. What we remember has already been affected by imagination when it moves into storage in our brains. When we recall a memory, imagination again plays a crucial role.

Our memories influence how we see both our past and our future. When we carry stored memories of predominantly pain and shame, it is difficult to imagine a future of hope for ourselves. David Hogue writes, "Recalling limiting or painful memories may prompt the brain to imagine future stories of hopelessness."[13] While we carry and deal with shameful memories, it is difficult to imagine a future that is positive and hope filled. When we have confessed shameful secrets, we may be freed to replace our imagination of a future of fear with more positive expectations. Painful memories can be transformed into positive futures when our imagination is opened to new possibilities. We may be able to imagine a future that is hopeful even when our memories are negative and painful and not filled with joy and comfort.

Part III: The Three Acts of Memory and Nothing Objective about Them

Researchers continue pursuing questions of what happens with different kinds of memory loss and how the mind works. We are learning more and more about memory, especially with the use of neuroimaging that takes the researcher into the brain to see where, when, and how memory functions. Even so, there is still a lot we don't know about memory.[14]

From our own experiences we do know that memory functions in three phases: The *perception* of the experience, the *storage* of the experience, and the *recall* of the experience. Each of these acts of memory has potential for creating distortion. At each step we may find ways to defend and help ourselves deal with the memories we carry and with those life events that created the memories.

Perception

Talk with any family member, friend, or colleague with whom you have shared a specific experience. Carefully compare what happened in each of your perceptions of the experience. The accounts will *never* be identical. In fact, they could diverge surprisingly. This enquiry could be done among persons who have just listened to the same sermon. Experienced preachers are often surprised by what some parishioners take away from their sermons. Each person's perspective is dramatically influenced by many factors at any given time and therefore affects what we preserve as memories. Shifting perspectives affect what our memories preserve.

When we hear a particular word, that word can call to mind a hot-button issue, and we "leave the moment" to follow our own thinking about the issue. We are listening to someone's story, and it reminds us of an experience of our own. We leap into remembering our own story. Someone shares a struggle they are having, and we race ahead to think up a solution or some reassurance and consequently stop hearing the account of *their* struggle. At these moments we lose what is happening with the other person. Our memory of the event itself is *significantly diminished.* In a sense, we were "not there." Memories hold our own reactions and may only vaguely capture and hold "real events," especially when we have lost focus on what has happened.

When we function on automatic, our perceptions of the experiences we have are not likely to remain clearly in our memories.[15] We have not perceived what has been happening with sufficient attention for it to register clearly in our memory. A good example of this experience is when we return to a parking lot without a clue about where we left the car. We do not fully or accurately recall what took place because our perception of it was limited. Our attention was not focused. Memory fails us at the moment of perception.

Our experiences as individuals, our histories, our contexts, and our self-interests all affect how we perceive everything that we experience. Therefore, we create our memories out of our particular focus on an event and not independently out of some actual objective event that comes to and remains in our memories, unaffected by our perception of the event and the way we have stored it.

Several years ago I went with a group of colleagues to see an opera performed by the Chicago Lyric Opera Company. A modernization of a famous opera, the story was set in a different time and place from its original setting. During one scene a number of naked women appeared on stage. There was no pretense of trying to hide their nakedness. Later, as several of us discussed the opera with others who had not been there, this scene came up. One of my colleagues who had been with us at the opera was *absolutely certain* that it did not happen. He was not ready to see naked women on stage, so he *did not* see them. There were several of us who had seen the women, so our perceptions checked with one another. We all distort our seeing and hearing in ways similar to this experience. Distortions in what we see mean distortions in what we remember. (I understand that our colleague did go back to see the opera again—checking up on our perceptions and memories, I presume.)

Storage

As we hold the event or experience in our memory, what happens to the memory as it is held there? Remembering, recall, and memory do not involve clear-cut matters. Memory researcher Daniel L. Schacter reflects that although we might expect it to do so, memory does not function like a photograph.[16] Experience is not taken like a photograph that then remains available as a replica of the original experience just as it was in our original perception of it. Schacter's judgment assumes a basic processing of the photo.

Storage becomes an even more complicated matter when we realize, as research tells us,[17] that pieces of particular memories are stored in different places in the brain, coming together only when "re-membered." One brain theory suggests that the brain determines which particular scattered pieces belong together in the act of remembering when the pieces have the same time of origin—when they arrived in the brain. This ability in recalling is still a mystery.[18]

I propose that memories may be more like photographs than Schacter suggested. Today, especially with digital photography, there can be many distortions of the original image created after the photo has been taken. Early in the history of photography, those processing film began to alter images taken and captured on film. In processing as well as in the taking of a photograph, new images were created. Double exposures, enlargement of a portion of the picture, photos set up to fool the eye, air brushing, and many tricks can be done that make a picture unlike the objective subject of the original photograph.

Now, by computer, those with the necessary technical skills are able to make photography much more like the experience of memory. The photographed images are manipulated, and additional images can be imported from another source. The photo result is not the image that was first shot. The memory recalled, like the processed photo, is not necessarily the true picture of the experience.

Even when we have a clear photo, unaltered, we may lose clarity regarding the names of the people or places in the photo, and forget the event it had captured. Over time photos fade, lose their vibrant colors, and the images they once captured begin to vanish.

A person who has a traumatic experience and holds it in their memory may do a great deal with it while it is held there. Highly emotional memories are most unlikely to go away.[19] Memories that are pain- and shame-filled demand a great deal of "gate keeping" energy to prevent us from remembering them, to restrain them from being recalled, and especially, from being revealed. The memory requires our attention to hide it so it will not overtake our thinking nor be discovered. But we remain concerned that secret memories will be exposed, found out; that what we remember will be discovered.

As they struggle with memory, some recreate, revisit, relive, rehearse, and review the memory on various levels while they try to keep it hidden as a secret in their lives. Some perpetrators of serious crimes are compelled to return to the scene of the crime over and over. We have similar behaviors with our memories. Memories also may return over and over in dreams with altered form and substance, still recognizable to the keeper, if not precise in actual events, than in accurate feelings from the events. Others who experience trauma such as childhood sexual abuse make a choice (not necessarily a conscious choice) not to remember the experience. The memory may be held sufficiently below the surface of consciousness so that it will emerge only when there is a powerful cue related to the event that forces it to mind. The details may change, but what remains is the basic experience of the event.[20]

When memories are kept hidden from the keeper, they may be stored in the keeper's body as a *body memory*. Our bodies hold memories of smell, sound, touch, and sight related to events that may at some time become cues for recall of a memory. Any one of these memories held in our body may at some time be triggered by a sensory experience that connects to the experience of what is stored in our memory. I am startled whenever I get a smell that immediately takes me back to South Africa, or a particular truck smell that reminds me of my days hitchhiking in Europe. Smell memories are extremely powerful and persistent. Other sensory-linked memories carry comparable power.

Similar to the act of perception, storage is not objective. We can alter our memories to fit how we see ourselves or how we want others to see us. We cannot rely on our memories to be objective. Our survival interests and context influence each act of memory. These influences should not be understood as necessarily negative. Acts of memory—perception, storage, and recall—work together and separately serving to help and protect us. Every act of memory can participate in distortion.

Recall

The events of storage and recall overlap. How a memory is stored and what is done with it while it is in storage determines to some extent how it is remembered, what is remembered, or if it is recalled at all. Recall can refer to memories I do not know I have, however, this book focuses mainly on those memories people know—at some level—they have. In the process of discussing the recall of memories, we need to give some attention to the recall of memories we have forgotten that we remember.

Miroslav Volf urges us to *redeem* our memories of wrongs suffered using these steps: "Remember truthfully!" "Remember therapeutically!" and "Learn from the past!"[21] His deepest concern is that healing and reconciliation come from remembering. He challenges us to live in accord with what we learn from our remembered experiences. He sees truthful recall as movement toward reconciling that will affect the whole society. We see from this discussion that what Volf recommends is not easy to do.

We are at different times defended and helped by each of these acts of memory along with the persistent potential our memory has for distorting each act it carries. All of us are capable of distorting our pasts.[22] Sometimes our memories are complicit in these acts of distorting to serve positive purposes.

Part IV: Can Memory Be Trusted?

The question of whether memory can be trusted to be true is a concern as we prepare ourselves to hear confessions. Raising this question is not intended to create mistrust of the person who confesses nor mistrust of memories confessed. Hogue recommends a receptive stance that includes both respect and suspicion.[23] It is realistic and faithful to recognize that we can do both.

When Memory Surprises

The recall of a memory that we have forgotten we remember may cause both confusion and anger. "If this is a real memory, then where has it been and what is wrong with me that I didn't remember it all along?" "Who could believe that happened, after all this time?" The keeper of the memory is puzzled about the absence of the memory— even when the hiddenness of the memory was functioning effectively to protect the memory keeper and perhaps other people who were involved. Puzzlement can be combined with relief as the keeper of the memory begins to recognize the role the kept memory has played in their life. Feelings about the original experience emerge with the memory and may add to existing shame, confusion, and anger about the unexpected memory.

Memories surprise us when we are given a cue that hooks us into the memory. Some traumatic experiences are only brought up out of our memories when a specific and sufficient cue is presented that touches off the memory. A young professional woman told me a story about her recall of a traumatic experience that she had not remembered until she experienced such a cue.

She was attending the funeral of an aunt, when her uncle, the husband of the deceased, greeted her with a kiss on the lips. At the moment of the kiss, she had an instant recall (flashback) of how that uncle had sexually abused her when she was a child. This flash of memory reminded her of what she had "forgotten." The cue of the kiss was strong enough and on target enough to bring back the vulnerability, anger, and shameful feelings she experienced in her suffering of abuse many years earlier. She had stored her traumatic experience as a body memory.[24]

Many cues that bring about recall are related to our senses. We see, hear, touch, feel, smell, or taste something that rocks us back to the experience. If this woman's uncle had just kissed her on the cheek, maybe she would not have received a cue sufficient enough to recall the forgotten memory. It may have been that only a kiss on her lips would be close enough to the past traumatic experience to enable her lost memory to return to consciousness.

In this situation the association of a physical cue and the setting of a funeral combined to allow the surfacing of the memory. Family gatherings, birthdays, weddings, holidays, the birth of a child, hospitalizations, deaths, and funerals are occasions ripe for remembering what we have forgotten that we remember. Ministers are present at many of these opportune occasions. Being present when the memory of an experience emerges may put us in the position to be seen as persons who could hear this newly unearthed secret.

The woman's recall possibly was able to take place because in addition to the cue in the kiss and the setting of the family gathering, she had experienced some significant success and was feeling a degree of comfort in her adult life. An experience of comfort or stability may contribute to the possibility that a forgotten memory can surface. Perhaps we unknowingly say to ourselves, "Now, I think I can handle it."

Even so, the memory may not be easy to face or to deal with regardless of the person's present level of comfort, feelings of strength, or satisfaction with life. In fact, the recall may be all the more surprising and disturbing because of stable life circumstances. Feeling a hard-won sense of security, a person who suddenly recalls a traumatic lost memory may be thrown off balance. Questions of what the memory means to current relationships and self-image become important. Is there anyone to whom she could confess this secret?

Memories Never Lost

In situations like that of my mother, presented earlier, I suspect that there was never a time when she had forgotten her traumatic abuse. She readily offered the secret to me when I revealed my negative feelings toward her father. My admission opened the door for her. I also realize that she had probably come to the place where she saw me as able to hear her secret. There was no suggestion, leading, or directing her into thinking she had been abused. Her experience is like that of many adults who keep secrets of childhood abuse. Memories like hers hang around, not out of reach, but just out of sight, tucked away from the eyes of anyone else. There can be little reason to doubt the truth of my mother's shared memory.

The Reality of False Memories

In contrast to the way my mother's secret was suddenly revealed, Volf illustrates what has been labeled a *false memory*:

> A person may remember that as a child he was mistreated by his father, though that idea has been planted in his mind by someone else, say, a misguided therapist. Is he remembering? Though he

believes he is remembering, he is not. We cannot remember what has not happened, and if we sincerely claim to remember a fictitious event, then strictly speaking we do not remember falsely, but instead falsely *believe* we remember what is a product of imagination.[25]

Volf goes on to elaborate on what came to be known as "False Memory Syndrome." Some adults, as a result of therapeutic suggestions, "recovered" memories of having been sexually abused by their parents. Their parents denied the real origins of their memories and sued the therapists. The problem that resulted from therapist-induced memories provided an escape for some parents who in reality *had* abused their children. They could then claim that the memories reported by their children were suggested and not real. Some children wrongly accused their parents of abuse, causing great trauma for the family with broken relationships and alienation.[26]

When a memory has long been hidden and suddenly emerges, the concept of false memory can be used to cause the person who remembers to doubt themselves and to lead them away from seeking someone to whom they could tell their secret. They experience even more shame. I tend to believe in the reality of spontaneously recalled memories. We need ways to enable people who may fear further embarrassment and ensuing family conflict to trust confessing their secret.

Persistence in Memory

Some memories are very troubling when the recall cannot be turned off. These memories are ones that we cannot help reliving. Traumatic events are usually the sources of these memories. They reappear again and again in images we see in our minds. Even though they are not real current events, the memories are vivid and overwhelming. At some points in one's life they might not be as present as at other times, but current life events may turn old memories into an urgent concern.

Military personnel who suffer from Post Traumatic Stress Disorder (PTSD) have terrifying flashbacks touched off by sounds or events that remind them of moments of danger from their deployment experiences.[27] PTSD is not limited to military experiences. Traumas of other kinds also initiate PTSD intrusions. Life circumstances provide situations that agitate old memories, making them harder to ignore and keep to one's self. They barge uncontrollably into the person's current life.[28] Traumatic memory flashbacks may cause disturbing behavior in the one remembering, including spouse abuse and other violent behaviors. The memories have been there all along, but particular life events cause them to emerge and make them more disturbing and difficult to hide and to control. Experience from the past intrudes into the present and the person remembering reacts as though they are present reality.

The Power of Suggestion and Memory's Unreliability

Recall is also affected by suggestion. What we recall of memories can be altered significantly when someone makes suggestions about what we experienced. Cases of mistaken identification by witnesses, and subsequent instances of overturned convictions, tell us that we must be cautious about how we ask others about their memories in life determining situations.

A Case of Misattribution

When I was in college a friend and I traveled to Europe one summer. It was a very low-budget production, and our transport around Europe was hitchhiking and biking. A few years after this trip, a seminary professor with whom I was studying gave the assignment to write a description of strong feelings experienced during some life event.

For this assignment I wrote about the experience of being on my bike speeding downhill in a small town in France. At the bottom of the hill was an intersection. As I approached that intersection a bus pulled in front of me crossing into the intersection and stopping right where my bike was headed. I put on my brakes as hard as I could. Although I started to slow down, I still was not going to stop in time. My bike was loaded with everything I was carrying for the summer and I was seconds and inches away from plowing into the side of the bus.

It was not until I had completely finished writing the paper describing my experience that I recognized that the event had never happened. I had written about my feelings of terror and helplessness and my awareness of the space narrowing between the front of my bike and the side of the bus. It was a vivid memory. This very vivid memory actually had been a dream I had while we were in Europe, but it lived in my mind as a terrifying memory from reality.

If I had not kept a journal, I might not have discovered that this experience was a dream rather than reality. I surprised myself with this distortion in my recall. I did not intend to deceive, and I can think of no purpose to this particular trick of my memory; but I had actually, temporarily deceived myself. I had almost unintentionally led my professor to believe a dream had been an actual event. After my realization and at the end of the paper I admitted my discovery. The question remains, can memory be trusted?

This distortion of memory falls into the category of *misattribution* identified by Schacter as one of the "seven sins of memory." Misattribution involves the assignment of a memory to the wrong source.[29] This distortion of memory can lead to serious problems when it occurs in situations that involve the vital accuracy.

Trusting Memories

This chapter may raise doubts about whether memories can be trusted. This book asserts that we can trust secrets people remember and confess. A lot of what is presented here points toward doubting the trustworthiness of our memories. How can these two, doubt and trust, exist together? Our tendency is to see doubt as bad and trust as good, but we have to live with both in every aspect of life.

It is necessary for children to trust their parents, but if they trust completely and never doubt, children will not grow up with trust in themselves. A child who grows up with complete trust absent of doubt will not be safe in a world in which there are both people and things that must not be trusted. In some life situations, doubt may mean safety and survival.

Memories create us, maintain us, and give us a sense of trust and security. Without memories we cannot feel secure. We literally do not know whether we are coming or going. In *Memento*, the movie mentioned earlier, one scene opens with Leonard running, and we hear him ask himself, 'What am I doing?" He spots another man running parallel to him, with a row of recreational vehicles lined up between them. They see one another as they pass the gaps between the RVs. He thinks he is chasing the man, but when he turns toward the man, the man shoots at Leonard. "No, he's chasing me." Leonard has no idea why he is running or who the other man is. We rely on memories to carry us through life experiences and actually to tell us whether we are coming or going and why, essential information we need in order to function in life.

We rely on our memories to carry the substance of our experiences, in many cases, over the span of years. Research on memories has revealed that the basic memories of particularly traumatic events are very likely to be remembered. Those memories laden with shame are the ones we must trust to be true (even when memory of details may be flawed) if we are to be able to come to terms with them and begin healing.

Memory has evolved within humanity in ways that help us survive. Studies of animals demonstrate that what they retain in their memories is geared to assist in their survival. This is also true for us. Our minds are designed to forget much of what we experience or we would be overburdened with remembering not only the events, but especially with experiencing the feelings those events carried with them. We do remember, however, much that we do not need, and perhaps that is because our evolution carries an expectation that some things will be needed for which we do not now find a purpose.

With all of that is riding on our memories; we recognize how memory can also be capricious and unreliable—at best confusing. What do we trust in our memories and in the memories of others that they reveal to us? Hogue's suggestion of "respect and suspicion" may help us, but it does not give us substantial answers. We also recognize that our memories are constantly at work—without our awareness, much of the time—as they distort some things that we hold in our memories, and function in other amazing ways to protect us. There is much we prefer not to remember, whether as it truly was or as we have remembered it to be.

Conclusion

At odd times I will have a flash of an image, a driveway in which we turned the car around in Lesotho when we were looking for a friend's family, a bit of path I have walked in San Anselmo, the back walk to a house where I lived in New Jersey. All of these images I have revisited at one time or another with no apparent connection or purpose. I wonder about these bits of images from my memory. Why have *these* been saved? And even more so, why do they come back to me at mysterious times, unconnected, as far as I can tell, to any current experience. How many more bits and pieces are there just tucked away in my memory, and for what purpose? These snatches of memory tell me that I do not know the depth or the breadth of my memory.

Alexander McCall Smith, in his interesting and beautiful novel set in Botswana, *The No. 1 Ladies' Detective Agency*, provides an answer to my question about the bits and pieces that surface unbidden. McCall Smith puts these words into the mouth of the novel's heroine, Mma Ramotswe:

> Our heads may be small, but they are as full of memories as the sky may sometimes be full of swarming bees, thousands and thousands of memories, of smells, of places, of little things that happen to us and which come back, unexpectedly, *to remind us of who we are.*[30] (Emphasis mine)

Leonard agrees with Mma Ramotswe when he says, "We all need memories to remind us of who we are." Memory serves us well, even with its limits, errors, and mysteries. Memories remind us of who we are, a very important task.

We must, after all, trust memory and seek to work with it—both seeing its flaws and recognizing its importance. Truly it is hard to live without memory and, just as truly, we cannot easily live with some of our memories.

In relation to secrets kept, memories are our means of holding secrets. Shameful memories that we hold as secrets are part of us. They do not have to be objective reproductions of actual experience in order to be painful and shameful to us. They can emerge from real-life experience, be altered by merger with memories of other experiences, by suggestion from others, by shifts in details, and by other distortions our memories create. Nevertheless, the pain and hurt of traumatic memories and secrets remain real and true.

As Leonard says, memory is our interpretation of an experience. Being an interpretation does not invalidate the memory. When a memory hurts and burdens our experience, it creates a need for confession and healing. On this occasion, questions about the accuracy of a memory are not primary. Healing is not dependent on proof of the factuality in the details of memory. Healing depends on someone hearing *the reality of the shame* which the secret keeper experiences. Healing also depends on someone *hearing the way in which the memory has functioned in the life of the keeper.*

Confessions bring to us all kinds of bits of life stored in memories. We hear and recognize all the possible distortions that may have played a role in what we hear. As we listen we do so, in our better moments, with both suspicion and respect. We do so with the hope that the faith we hold may be able to speak to those whose secrets we hear—that we are helping them remember truthfully and move toward reconciliation and renewal in their lives.

Chapter 7

From Generation to Generation

The Power of Secrets in the Church

Introduction

Not surprisingly, secrets are kept over generations. Both families and churches pass on again and again the damaging effects of secrets. It is not the secret itself that gets passed on but its effects. The secret itself is a kept secret. What is passed on is the urgency of keeping the secret. Some persons living with the consequences of unrecognized secrets within congregations and within families do not even know that secrets exist. They live with dynamics that they do not understand. These dynamics may continue in effect for many years without anyone acknowledging what lies beneath them. As long as the secret is underground, the destructive legacy can remain.

We begin with David and Bathsheba and then continue with the story of Tamar, daughter of David. Efforts required to keep secrets have consequences far beyond the secrets themselves. Struggles to keep secrets bind families in painful places and distort relationships and lives.

The biblical story of David and his family demonstrates how people work at keeping shameful secrets at any cost. In David's family, the result is the loss of one life after another and ongoing alienation within the family. The similarity in our lives is most poignant in words describing Tamar as a "desolate woman," an experience repeated over and over even until today.

In addition to the family, the church is a place in which we discover many secrets sheltered by what may even seem to be conspiracies. *Keeping secrets is often more damaging than experiences that created the secrets in the first place.*[1] Secrets not confessed continue in the lives of families and churches in the form of destructive behaviors that function to assure that the secret will not be exposed. How are individuals in the congregation to be freed from perpetuating the destruction of kept shameful secrets? This question informs the direction of this chapter.

Part I: Kept Secrets Lead to Destruction

Beginnings in One Generation

The desire to maintain power, image, name, and respect drives the need to keep secrets hidden. Holders of secrets believe what they value would be destroyed if the secret were revealed, so much has to be done to keep the secret hidden.

David's story of betrayal that initiates his secret keeping begins in 2 Samuel 11. As he strolls around on his roof, looking down on the surrounding neighborhood, David notices a beautiful woman bathing. This woman is not only beautiful, but she is also unavailable. However, her husband, Uriah, happens to be off at war, a fact that alters her availability status in the eyes of the king. David is king, and for him this means both that he can take whatever he wants, without regard for his commitment to his God and his people, *and* that he must protect his image in the eyes of his people at all costs.

Out of his obsession for Bathsheba, David has her brought to the palace. He has sexual intercourse with her and then sends her back home. It does not appear that there is anything mutual about their relationship, but rather it is an act of power, violence, and rape, and it has to be kept secret.

Everything is just fine for David (the incident perhaps forgotten), until Bathsheba informs him that she is pregnant. Then David needs a plan to conceal his illicit behavior. At this point it becomes evident that the secret itself may be less problematic than the actions it demands in order to keep the secret. Also a part of the story is the *parenthetical* comment about Bathsheba's bathing. "(Now she had been purifying herself after her period)" (2 Samuel 11:4). Spoken so simply, the inclusion of this detail sets up complications that King David now faces to keep his original betrayal a secret. The baby can't possibly be Uriah's. David's need to keep his misconduct secret goes far beyond the secret itself when we see what he decides he must do to keep it.

Uriah being out of town both offers David an opportunity and now causes him a dilemma. David's first attempt to cover his recklessness is to order Uriah to come home with a report of how the battle is going with the plan to get him to have sexual intercourse with his own wife. Nothing stops David from doing what he thinks will help him hold onto his power and image. All of David's trickery fails and Uriah's integrity prevails. Uriah won't have sex with his wife. Instead, he returns to the battlefront and David (a king now without faithfulness or integrity) sends a message, *with Uriah, by his own hand,* giving instructions to Joab to set up Uriah so he will be killed. David's plan to save his own position in the sight of others requires that he arrange for Uriah to be murdered. He exhibits no concern about collateral damage in the loss of lives of other troops.

Biblical commentator, Anderson, offers this reflection:

> Thus the death of Uriah appears nearly pointless while the callous scheme itself becomes exceedingly despicable. It is ironic in the extreme that the one who ought to be the guardian of the people's rights and justice should murder his loyal servant and cause the deaths of other faithful soldiers in order to protect the façade of his honor which he himself had already disgraced.[2]

When David receives word about the battle and Uriah's death, he sends reassurance to Joab, noting that it was a battle and some get killed and he should press on to victory. In particular David's words deny his plan for Uriah's death, "Do not let this matter trouble you."[3] He will speak similar words later.

The story continues with David taking Bathsheba as his wife, followed by the confrontation of David by the prophet Nathan. Where there is any doubt about wrongdoing, Nathan makes it clear. He tells David a story about a rich man with many sheep taking a poor man's only lamb (that "was like a daughter to him") to slaughter in order to feed a traveler who had come to him. David is outraged by the rich man's behavior (doing what he could do because he had power?) and says the man should die. Nathan's response is, "You are that man!" Nathan continues, "This is what the LORD says: I am making trouble come against you *from inside your own family*" (2 Samuel 12:11, emphasis mine). Nathan tells David that God will let him live, but that the child will die. None of this, even the illness and death of the son born to Bathsheba, leads David to reconsider his need to keep his secret hidden.

The great lengths to which David will go in order to keep his secret hidden give us a picture of how deeply secret keepers are affected by their shameful secrets and how much their need not to be exposed controls their lives. One thing David knows is that keeping his secret will mean that he keeps his power.[4]

The Next Generation

Amnon, son of David, next in line to the throne, half-brother of Tamar, is filled with lust for Tamar to the point of making him ill. His friend and cousin Jonadab is crafty and develops a plan for Amnon to get his hands on his beautiful sister. King David is enlisted to order Tamar to go to Amnon's place and fix him some cakes. David is convinced that this would be just what Amnon needs to feel better. David sends Tamar into disaster as he sent Uriah to death.

Tamar obeys her father, unknowingly putting herself at risk. Deception brings Tamar into Amnon's quarters and, despite her objections, he grabs her, "and he laid her."[5] The deception has been effective for Amnon's purposes, and another shame-filled secret comes into being. Secrecy and violence span generations: David *takes* Bathsheba and Amnon *lays* Tamar. Amnon replicates his father's behavior. Where secrets are hidden, similar dynamics often emerge.

Amnon's feelings of loathing for Tamar, after raping her, exceed the passion he had for her prior to the rape. He has her thrown out of his quarters ("send *this* away"[6]) and the door locked behind her, leaving her with her shame and in public, crying in her torn princess robe with her hand and ashes on her head—traditional expressions of grief. In these moments she is in public with her pain and despair. So far, she still has a voice, but this soon comes to an end when she is silenced.

Their brother, Absalom, seeing her condition, asks Tamar, "Has your brother Amnon been with you? Keep quiet about it for now, sister; he's your brother. Don't let it bother you" (13:20).[7] Absalom minimizes Tamar's pain and humiliation, telling her to keep the secret. Tamar is effectively silenced. "So Tamar remained, a desolate woman, in her brother Absalom's house" (13:20 NRSV).[8] For Tamar there would be no voice, no marriage, no children, no respect, no place, except for her space in her brother's house—as a "desolate woman."[9] We cannot count how many women since Tamar have become such desolate women!

The image of Tamar as a desolate woman for the rest of her life is an image of a woman carrying the shameful burden of a secret she cannot speak and from which she cannot be released. Even though King David, her father, learns what has happened and is enraged, he does nothing. Birch offers this reflection on the consequences of David's behavior, "Perhaps David is so morally compromised by his own flagrant crimes that he cannot confront the excesses of his sons...and in doing so he unwittingly allows Absalom's murderous rage to run its course."[10]

With kept secrets there are repercussions across generations, throughout families. Absalom did not forget Amnon's rape of their sister. He developed a plan for Amnon's murder. Like his father, Absalom ordered others to do his killing for him.[11] Absalom promised he would take the blame. The consequences of David's behavior become evident: "Now David's two oldest sons have repeated his actions: One has taken for himself the object of his sexual desire, and the other has killed for the sake of his own personal and political interests."[12] The score in King David's family is now two rapes and two murders (as well as the death of a child and unnecessary deaths of some of David's army). These events are necessitated by having to do whatever it takes to keep secrets hidden.

At first, David thinks all of his sons are dead, but then gets word that only Amnon is dead. Jonadab, David's nephew and army commander, steps up, reminding David about Absalom's resentment about the rape of Tamar,[13] offering assurance that only Amnon is dead (13:32). Absalom then flees to Geshur (his maternal homeland) where he remains for three years, leaving David to mourn for the death of Amnon and the absence of Absalom.

Joab perceives that David longs for Absalom and sends for a "wise woman" to carry a message back to David. His effort is meant to persuade David to receive Absalom back in Jerusalem. The woman does her job well, telling a parable-like story about her "two sons." One son had killed the other and her plea is for the king to remove a death sentence for her other son. David supports her wish and says she would not see the death of her second son. David also sees through her story and recognizes Joab's hand in her visit and story. Bruggemann offers us a helpful understanding that David seems to miss: "When the cycle of vengeance is broken, homecoming is possible . . . for an instant the woman has permitted him to perceive life in an alternative way. Vengeance is never broken until life is discerned differently."[14] But even though David receives Absalom back to Jerusalem as a result of the wise woman's/Joab's parable, he does not take advantage of the promised path to true reconciliation that her tale offered. The king's response is, "Let him go to his own house; he is not to come into my presence" (14:24 NRSV). David's response is only half-hearted, and he misses an

132

opportunity for breaking the cycle of secrets and violence carried in his family. There is no reconciliation, no restoration. Tragedy continues, and Absalom's death at the hands of Joab and Joab's men is next.

Secrets kept by David, Tamar, Amnon, and Absalom lead to the deaths of Uriah, the first baby born to David and Bathsheba, Amnon, and finally, Absalom. Even the tragedy of Tamar is much like death; with no husband she has no future prospects for living a full life. The first response to each event is silence and inaction. When actions are finally taken, they result in violence and further division.

David's story ends without the secrets being faced. The deaths mount up and Tamar leads a life close to death. This cycle could have been interrupted. At different times persons involved could have taken action to interrupt the painful direction in which events are heading. Maintaining secrecy and an inability to see circumstances in a new way compound the potential for continued violence and destruction. The threat of their exposure drives David and his sons to do whatever is necessary to avoid disclosure of their secrets. Even though the wise woman sent to David by Joab was able to offer a story that imagined "vengeance could be forgone in favor of compassion,"[15] David was unable to receive the blessing of her offer to allow reconciliation to take over from vengeance, secrecy, violence, and division. He could not envision that what he had done could be turned around and healed.

The wise woman's story offers us the same opportunity to tell the truth and be freed from the shame of past secrets.[16] Her story offered to David also reveals that taking a step out of shame and violence requires compassion. When shame demands our silence, we fail to reach for the hope that is possible in our lives.

Part II: The Church: Secrets from Generation to Generation

Reconciliation can take the place of violence and division. Both Nathan and the wise woman offer us images of how such stories can lead to healing and reconciliation when the truth is told. While secrets remain untold, the destruction that comes from efforts to keep the secrets continues. The experience of being part of a community can offer an antidote for shame, so one could expect that the church would be the ideal place for the elimination or prevention of secrets. The problem is that churches can fail to offer genuine community. This happens when the church is preoccupied with things it must do to maintain, promote, and protect its image.

When secrets remain untold the destruction that comes from efforts to hide the secrets continues. True human communities of hospitality and humility offer places where secrets can be revealed and the secret keeper released from his or her bondage and all that is required to be able to hide the secret. We expect that the church can be the place that offers community, but too often the church fails at being this kind of true community.

When leadership fails to preach sermons or teach classes on stories that shine revealing light on shameful secrets in scripture, like David's rape of Bathsheba and Tamar's rape by Amnon,[17] people cannot benefit from David's mistakes and his continued failure to interrupt the chain of secrecy that helped destroy his family. When we learn about and recognize David's disastrous secret keeping, maybe we will see the secrets we keep in a new light and with greater understanding. Our avoidance of these biblical stories contributes to the church continuing to hold shameful secrets and pass them along from one generation to another.

A church hiding secrets becomes dysfunctional, and anger becomes predominant in its interpersonal dynamics. Visitors, sensing something in the air, may feel unwelcome. How can they be welcome when every additional person increases the threat of discovery of the secret? New ministers are met with walls of mistrust, hostility, and rebellion, or they are sought out to be coconspirators who will not challenge the existing system. Sexual and fiscal misconduct by church leaders are common secrets churches hold with shame and carry with fear of exposure. While someone who is long gone may have caused the shame, the shame still lingers on as shame owned by everyone in the church, even when they do not know the origins of the secret. The church is bound by the shame of the secret. What the church needs to recognize is how much can be gained when a secret is confessed and there is reconciliation with the truth.

One Church among Many

An interim pastor I will call Jeanne told about her experience in what she understood from the start was a difficult church. When she began her ministry, denominational authorities did not tell her anything about past or existing problems in the church. Quickly, she met obvious resistance to her ministry. She discovered on her own that the tenure of her predecessor had been relatively brief, as had been the terms of the two pastors preceding him. No one had given her this information. Through examination of church records she realized that a large number of church members had ceased to attend and contribute to the church. But there was also no record of their uniting with other churches or of anyone having visited them to discover why they left.[18]

Pastor Jeanne began to be suspicious that there might have been some occurrence of ministerial misconduct. When such misconduct occurs, especially sexual misconduct, the efforts to keep it secret result in many negative patterns, such as the pattern Benyei observes: "A frequently observed pattern, usually resulting from clergy misconduct, is the *clergy killer congregation.* These congregations express the pain of their organizational distress through a history of short-term pastorates and an air of anti-clericalism."[19] Congregations find it extremely difficult to trust new clergy when they have experienced the extreme betrayal of sexual misconduct.

After several months in this new ministry and after persistently asking questions about the church's history (for which she was rebuffed or misled), she built tentative relationships with a few church leaders. She was aware of their discomfort with her questions and, yet, that they were cautiously finding their way to trust her. After some time, a couple of the leaders decided that she should know what had happened but that no one outside of their circle should find out. Pastor Jeanne was being enlisted into the group working to keep the secret. Much to the dismay of the leaders who told her the secret, Pastor Jeanne decided that she could not agree to their demand to keep the secret along with them. She felt, first of all, that the life of the church was at risk in doing so. Even though the leaders were distraught, she did not weaken. Her convictions demanded a lot of courage, and she drew on the courage she knew she had. She was clear that all the members of the church needed to know. As long as they did not know the concealed secret, the whole church acted out of discomfort, grief, anger, fear, and confusion. The church's ministry and mission were trapped, with its future in question.

Pastor Jeanne could see all the walls that had been built within the church and around the church. The intent was to keep the image of the church positive and the problems within hidden. There were obvious barriers to certain issues being discussed. The primary concern of the lay leadership was the protection of the church's reputation. How could they recognize the behavior of the pastor's betrayal and still be a valued church community?

Mystery writer Louise Penny offers this relevant reflection from her lead detective, "Armand Gamache knew that no good ever came from putting up walls. What people mistook for safety, was in fact captivity."[20] This seems close to the church's experience of kept secrets. Walls that prevent the confession and subsequent working through the issues related to the secret hold the church in captivity—preventing the church's full performance of its mission. Thus, we are not protected but hampered.

Because of the clear lines between those who knew and those who could not know, there were strong divisions within the church. Those who were in power consistently denied these divisions. Painful feelings went underground and remained there. Jeanne recognized the anger of the leaders toward her, because of her refusal to comply with their expectations that she join them in secret keeping. She knew that anger also would be directed at the few leaders who had broken their bond of silence and control and told the secret. Pastor Jeanne saw all of this swirling around her in the church. But she remained resolute that they had to face the secret.

The Road toward Reconciliation and Renewal

Pastor Jeanne realized that there is no quick fix for the church's situation.[21] Merely revealing the secret to the people could be perceived as a quick fix. The presence of individual and family secrets within the community might also further complicate dealing with church secrets. The revelation of a church secret could pose a threat to members with secrets of their own, as they wonder, "Will mine be revealed, too?" When individual secrets are connected, or even at the heart of the church secret, we see how apparent the threat can be. If the secret indeed involved clergy sexual misconduct, there may be a victim of this misconduct, or even more than one victim, whose involvement may be unknown. They might fear exposure if the pastor's misconduct is named.

Let me add further complications. Pastor Jeanne was an interim, which meant concern about keeping her position as pastor in this church was not as at-risk as it would be with a pastor in a regular position or appointment. She knew her role in this congregation was for a limited time period, which might allow her to be freer to take more risks. However, what if Pastor Jeanne had a secret herself that she had not faced? That could have possibly interfered with her response to this congregation. The pastor who holds an unresolved secret and faces a congregation's secret may find that her own secret leads her to feel threatened by the potential revelation of the church's secret. It does not need to be a similar secret for it to pose a threat. The fears of also becoming exposed may lead to hesitation or avoidance in dealing with the church's secret. This is not a logical connection. But happily in this case, Pastor Jeanne's level of comfort in dealing with the secret suggested that she was not holding a significant shameful secret.

Creating a Caring Congregation

Pastor Jeanne's decision not to tell the secret right away did not mean that she would not tell it later. Although she was not going to tell the congregation the secret she now knew, she had to do something else.

It couldn't be a quick fix because healing would have to involve trans-formation within the congregation. She wanted to see them become a community with characteristics that would allow them to incorporate their awful secret into their awareness and self-understanding, while still having strength and true self-esteem (both individually and com-munally). Because she enabled the church leaders to tell her the secret, she had already demonstrated that she had at least a basic character of leadership that could accomplish this. Something about her made that possible. Perhaps a strong level of emotional maturity was evident in how she related to the people.

First of all, Pastor Jeanne modeled for the people qualities that con-tributed to the creation of a true community. She chose not to jump into a fix-it mode, which demonstrated her *humility* and denied that she was seeking to focus on herself for her own advantage. Rather, she *sought the benefit of the people and the church*. She had been *open* to the people, *honest* ("I won't join with you to keep the secret."), *accepting,* and *nonjudgmental*. Her response to hearing the story was not to judge them for what a former pastor had done nor for keeping what he had done a secret nor for wanting her to keep the secret with them. She also demonstrated ability and wisdom to keep *appropriate boundaries*, again because she did not comply with their wish for her to join them in keeping the secret. She was appropriately *available,* enabling their growing trust in spite of the context of betrayal that would deny any trust. In all of her encounters with her congregation, Pastor Jeanne af-firmed the *worth of the people*—all the people. Valuing the people also included her effort to include everyone's participation in power in the congregation. They didn't want her to tell, so she did not make a uni-lateral decision to tell. She knew there was another way. Even though she did not tell, she also did not agree to keep the secret.

Pastor Jeanne saw the hope that was available and she was able to hold that hope for the people while they moved slowly toward it. Their movement necessitated their being able to incorporate what Pas-tor Jeanne modeled for them. Could they learn to be a community bearing those precious qualities that create true community?

Conclusion

Candace Benyei claims, "Most of the destructive behaviors of individuals, families, and institutions revolve around the attempt to preserve and bolster self-image at the expense of others, as well as maintain a position of felt security without regard for one's neighbor."[22] In this description we can see reflections of King David in all of his efforts to maintain his self-image without regard for life or well-being of anyone else. We also find these dynamics in churches. What Benyei describes is certainly true of the pastor who betrays a congregation with any form of misconduct. We want to see church leadership that is free from behavior that disregards others. We can only find that freedom from destructive behavior when we have leaders who have *appropriate regard for themselves*. We do not show disregard for others when we truly feel valued.

Chapter 5 offers us the spectrum of a balance between autonomy and shame. Neither extreme of autonomy nor of shame promises us an effective minister. It is within the context of balance that we find the qualities of a pastor who will be able to respond to the secrets people hold and not create more secrets for the church to live with in shame. Living with balance we recognize that we are limited beings and that we need each other. That is the image of the church as one body with all the different parts depending upon one another that we find in 1 Corinthians 12:14-26. Balance includes appropriate regard for self and for those different others who are in community with us. We are a community and not isolated individuals, as both autonomy and shame tend to mislead us.

Facing secrets and their extensive trails of destructive concealment, we look for alternatives to keeping damaging secrets that cause division and isolation.

Jesus' parable of the Prodigal Son "suggests that separation need not be the accepted reality. There can be return, forgiveness, and new beginnings."[23] Persons in ministry can hold and offer visions of hope for those carrying shameful secrets so that they can become free from their shame.

Chapter 8

Hearing Secrets as a Means of Grace

Introduction

Secret keepers are able to reveal secrets that were held in shame when there is a context that assures they will be heard. In many ways, persons in ministry see their work as enabling people to realize the grace of God. The ministry of receiving confessions is a part of this work. We help people move toward grace and love, as we receive confessions of secrets bound by shame, and people are able to share confessions when they find themselves in a community of hospitality.

In this chapter we turn to the parable of the Prodigal Son to see the love and grace of God as a way of preparing ourselves to be able to hear confessions, to help others recognize the reality of God's grace available to them, and to enable them to speak their secrets in safety. Surrounded by and assured of this grace and love, they are able to trust within the context we provide. *Our being available to hear sometimes horrible secrets and still treasure the secret keeper is essential to moving the secret telling toward becoming a means of grace.* This possibility involves who we are and not just what we do or what we say in ministry.

We will also be looking at the biblical story of Joseph and the way in which his betrayal by his brothers and the secret they kept about his fate are turned into an experience of grace when Joseph reveals the secret his brothers kept.

The preceding chapters introduced dynamics of painful secrets with an emphasis on shame as a common factor in secrets. We examined ways to interpret memory and lying when secrets are kept. Understanding these factors provides some first steps to help us become able to hear shameful secrets that may be told to us. We have considered who the person in ministry must be in order to welcome and receive secrets.

Part I: At the Heart of Receiving Secrets

A Foundation in the Grace of God

The familiar story of the Prodigal Son provides a theological foundation for caregivers both preparing to open doors for the telling of secrets and for their becoming able to hear secrets. We are able to come to God, in whatever mess we are in or as whatever mess we are, and be welcomed by God. That is what our faith tells us, and it may even be what we preach and teach. The faith we *practice*, however, reveals that we too often consider ourselves and others as unacceptable to God. We do not expect anything like the welcome reception the Prodigal Son received from his father—the father that we see as representing God.

I remember a conversation with a young pastor who was going through a very difficult time. As he talked, grace unexpectedly broke into the conversation when I thought to remind him that he was precious to God. He seemed stunned and, with tears in his eyes, expressed what that affirmation meant to him. However, the faith we demonstrate may stand as a barrier both to those who have secrets they want to tell and for those of us who want to be able to hear them. That pastor had lost touch with the message of his own valued status in God's sight. I suspect this loss is common for many persons in ministry.

We look at the story of the Prodigal Son to discover a path from the faith we practice regarding God's grace, to the incredible power of God's grace as seen in the father of the Prodigal Son. The words of Jesus about the Prodigal's father invite us to live out of the deep understanding of God's grace that we discover in the parable.

The Context for the Parable

Luke 15 opens with the Pharisees grumbling about Jesus, "This man welcomes sinners and eats with them" (v. 2). Jesus first responds to this judgment with two short stories. The first is about a lost sheep and the second is about a lost coin. In both stories the lost is sought and found and much rejoicing follows. The text compares the joy over what has been lost being found to a celebration in heaven over every found sinner (e.g., the sinners about whom the Pharisees complained). One could say that the celestial celebration is saturated with joy.

That which is valued is missed and a search initiated. The shepherd who has lost the sheep and the woman who has lost the coin set aside other matters—like the other ninety-nine sheep and demands of household duties—in order to search. To us, one lost coin and one sheep (when you have ninety-nine others) may not sound like big losses, but the inconsequentiality of what has been lost may be important as we consider the stories told here. The seekers become finders in these two searches. Great joy and celebration ensue; then we arrive at the parable of the Prodigal Son.

The rest of chapter 15 is the story of the lost son who is found by his father—this father who has two sons. Celebration follows, but we get an additional element in this story of the lost that is found—the response of the elder brother who refuses to join in the celebration of what was lost being found. As we contemplate this parable, we might examine the added element of the older brother and recognize in him the faith *we* may tend to practice.

The father in this story offers a joyful celebration for the clearly disrespectful son who he goes out to meet. However, the father meets the elder brother's complaints about the welcome-home staged for his little brother with just as much love and grace as he has for the Prodigal. The role this father plays challenges our view of God, who should be angry and ready to judge his son—actually, *both* sons.

Looking at the Parable

As the parable begins we learn from Jesus that we will be hearing about a father who has two sons. In the next verse our focus is directed away from the father to the younger son. I propose that our attention should remain with the father. The parable is about the father. *He* is the focus.[1] While we typically call this parable "the Prodigal Son," Jesus' story is actually about the Prodigal father. The word *prodigal* means extravagant to the point of bring wasteful, which characterizes the father's (God's) love. The name we give this parable actually directs us toward the younger son, "the Prodigal." We make the message of the parable easier on ourselves when we keep the younger son as our focus. The message about the father is about God's relationship with us. The elder brother is much like us people of faith.

The younger son makes an outrageous request of his father—that his father give him his inheritance now (instead of waiting until his father's death). Culturally this request is *so* out of order—totally unacceptable behavior, but amazingly, the father complies. The son gets his inheritance. This son's request for his inheritance is actually an insult to the father's honor, as is his leaving home with his father's fortune.[2] Within the next few days the son is gone to "a land far away" with all he now possesses. There he "wasted his wealth through extravagant living" (v. 13). The scripture gives us no other particulars about how he wasted his inheritance.

Soon his fortune is gone and the distant country slips into a famine. In desperation this son hires himself out in order to be able to survive. The job he gets is feeding pigs, which were considered taboo. Things couldn't get much worse for a young Jewish man far from home. But, they *do* get worse. He finds himself considering joining the pigs in what they are eating. And, sadly we read, "no one gave him anything."

While we reflect on this story, we keep in mind that he brought all this on himself, even though we may sympathize with him in his circumstances. It is his own fault.

Finally, this younger son comes "to his senses" and realizes that even his father's servants are better off than he is now.[3] He knows that at home he would be able to have enough to eat and decides to head there and offer himself as a servant in his father's house. He has no expectation of forgiveness and reinstatement as his father's son. He prepares a speech to deliver to his father as he sets off for home. We surmise that he is motivated by hunger more than anything else. Many scholars have questioned whether he was actually repentant,[4] but some agree that the expression "he came to his senses" indicates repentance.[5] However, the son's expectation is only that he could become a servant in his father's house and his concern is that he then would have food to eat. He does not anticipate reconciliation with his family. He does not expect restoration to his family role or place. What he has done goes far beyond whatever he could expect would be forgiven.

Another Kind of Reception

Years ago I saw an opera about the Prodigal Son. I was astonished by the way in which the homecoming scene was staged. In my memory, the father stands at the gate to his home. He looks very stern and stands with his arms crossed resolutely, unmovable. We see the weak, tattered, and hungry son crawl from stage left while the father barely looks at him, standing his ground. The son arrives at his father's feet clutching at his robes, imploring him for some reception. (Of course, both are singing all this time.) I was completely astonished about how far this depiction was from scripture's account! *This* image of the father, however, happens to be more faithful to the first century's cultural expectation of the father. The intent of the parable, though, is lost in this dramatization. We may actually be more comfortable with the opera's image of the father's harsh reception.

Notice this contrast. "While he was still a long way off, his father saw him and was moved with compassion. His father ran to him, hugged him, and kissed him" (v. 20). From our cultural perspective we do not recognize how the father was demeaning himself in taking this action. He further dishonored himself by showing his legs as he pulled up his robes to keep from tripping on them as he ran down the road to find his lost son.[6] In ancient Jewish culture, in welcoming his son so warmly, the father shamed himself. Unlike the opera depiction, the father makes himself look foolish and totally undignified. He loses all the honor of his social status. This son had disrespected him, and it was "beneath" the father's position to welcome him back home in this way, if at all.[7] There is more to this picture; by running to meet his son the father protected the son from any threat by villagers who would be ready to stand up for the father's lost honor by taking violent action against this returning, disrespectful son.[8]

The father's welcome was far beyond any expectation. An angry rejection would have been anticipated and seen as appropriate by the community.[9] The story is not as simple as the son coming back home. The son was dead to his father and was *found* by the father. The father's run down the road to greet his son after spotting him at a distance supports the image of the son being found.[10] In addition, the concept of the son being found is informed by the prior stories of the lost sheep and lost coin that are found and reflects the great joy expressed in the celebrations of their being found.

We notice that the father's welcome and joy precede any confession from the son. The image someone gave me was that the father was hugging him so tightly and kissing him, so he had no chance at first to give his planned speech. When the son gets free enough he offers his prepared speech that includes, "I no longer deserve to be called your son" (v. 21). We wouldn't even know from reading the text that the father heard a word he said.

The effusive welcome home and the joy of the father were evident before the son could say anything. This part of the story is worthy of closer attention because we may find trouble fitting it with our theologies. The father in this parable represents God. Jesus tells us that the welcome the son receives is what we are to expect *even before we seek welcome, forgiveness, or redemption.* The welcome is already ours![11] But, we don't act like we believe this—for ourselves or for anyone else— especially those we think we must judge or condemn. We seem to live to avoid punishment rather than act to express God's boundless love to others and expect it for ourselves. We know we don't deserve such love and neither did the Prodigal *or* his brother. Yet his father (like God) loved him even before he expressed any regrets or asked for forgiveness. We do not see the older son express any repentance for his attitude. Still, he too, is loved. This image challenges our theologies.

Remembering David's Reception of Absalom

The enthusiastic and loving welcome the Prodigal receives from his father is quite a contrast to the way in which David's long absent son, Absalom, was received (2 Samuel 14:33):

> The narrator's restraint in describing the encounter between David and Absalom suggests that Absalom's obeisance was decorous rather than deferential, and David's kiss was more perfunctory than purposeful.[12]

It is possible that "David may have been an expert in repentance (if Psalm 51 may truly be accorded to him), but he knew little of grace."[13] What a difference between the greetings of these two fathers! While Absalom's presence offered the opportunity for an expression of grace and an experience of reconciliation, none of this was available from King David. If David had taken to heart the tale of the wise woman sent by Joab (2 Samuel 14:1-20), he could have been open to a more gracious welcome of Absalom—and taken the opportunity to put an end to the chain of family secrets and violence. David could see the point of her story, but he could not take it to heart and live it out in his relationship with Absalom. David's reception leads instead to Absalom's proceeding to steal the hearts of the people of Israel from David (15:1-6). The character of the Prodigal (and his brother) and

Absalom may be more similar than not. Their return to their fathers is not remorseful but expedient. The issue is the character of the fathers. In *them* lies the difference between the receptions of their sons.

The Prodigal's Reception Continues

The father, immediately after finding his lost son, sets in motion preparations for a feast for a large number of people. He orders servants to bring the symbols of son-ship—the best robe, a ring, and sandals—none of which would be offered to the found son were he to return to take the role of a servant in the household.[14] "This son of mine was dead and has come back to life! He was lost and is found!" (Luke 15:24). The father expresses his powerful feelings of love and joy, his delight in reconciliation with his lost son. The father's behavior toward his sons is quite moving to the reader, *when we allow it.*

The celebration begins, and the elder son, coming in from the field where he was working, asks a servant what is going on. He learns that his brother has come home safe and sound and their father killed the fatted calf and is throwing him a big party. The elder brother's first response is resentment and anger. I can identify with the older brother's feelings. He is the hard-working and faithful son. He has been the one who has given honor due to his father. Why should the brother who betrayed the family, wasted his inheritance, and dishonored their father get any kind of welcome?

In order to get the elder son to come join the festivities, the father further dishonors himself by leaving his guests at the party he is throwing. Again, this is inappropriate behavior for the father—the father dishonoring himself. Then, in refusing to participate in the celebration, the older son multiplies the disrespect his father has already received from the younger son and the father's loss of honor in the community. The elder brother accompanies his refusal with an angry complaint, recounting his faithfulness and hard work and expressing his resentment for not having had any party thrown for him (not even with a goat)—the good son, who has done what is expected.[15] In his tirade, the elder brother even embellishes on the known facts, making his own assumptions about what his brother did with the lost inheritance.

The father responds with an extraordinary measure of acceptance, love, and grace that matches the reception he gave to the lost son. This crabby, self-righteous, angry son (reminiscent of the Pharisees at the beginning of Luke 15) is assuredly beloved by the father who tells him, "Everything I have is yours" (v. 31). The father reiterates the importance of the celebration for his younger son who was dead and is now alive, lost and now found. Even as he offers this explanation again, the father does not diminish his love and acceptance of his elder son.[16] We don't expect this. In fact, it is difficult for us to accept the words and behavior of this father. Our inability to believe the extent of the father's love may contribute to our preference for keeping the focus of the parable on the son.

God's Grace

God's boundless love is beyond our comprehension because it is so outrageous and excessive. The grace and love of God lie beyond our ability to grasp them. We are so limited by our own ability to love when others disappoint us, do wrong, or cause us shame. With the shame we hold, we see ourselves as unworthy. We transfer our limitations to our understanding of God and anticipate much more judgment and punishment than grace. Emil Brunner says, regarding this parable, "Were we really to grasp it with all our heart, our life would overflow with joy and love."[17] Instead, we miss what Jesus is trying to tell us in the image of the father in the Parable. The message Brunner reflects stands in contradiction to how we tend to see ourselves and one another in the sight of God—*especially before we even repent*. God's grace is, nevertheless, right there for us, seeking us out even before we get "home."

The Prodigal Father and Receiving Secrets

This parable's image of God's grace and boundless love available to us just as we are holds a key to our being able to respond to those who tell shameful secrets. This understanding of God's love, given to us through the words of Jesus, provides a foundation for our view of ourselves. When we see ourselves as so wildly loved by God— regardless—we are better equipped to convey to those who carry shameful secrets, that here is a place where they can speak and still be loved. We convey the depth and breadth of God's love to others when we believe it for ourselves.

We are able not only to find the lost but also, like the father, to risk our own dignity in order to find them. To hear painful secrets we have to be willing and able to be vulnerable, to risk listening to what we do not want to hear—to risk our honor to be with secret keepers in their "ugly" spaces. When we hear and receive a secret teller, we express the grace of God to them through the boundless love we find in the Prodigal's father and, in turn, offer to them. We stand with the speaker.

Part II: The Power of Being Heard

Hearing as Hospitality

Being heard is much like being received with a warm welcome, an offering of hospitality. Secret keepers are offered a "comfortable place to sit" and some "refreshment." Abraham and Sarah set the standard for hospitality, as they welcomed the strangers in the desert and gave them a place to rest and food to eat (Genesis 18). Emulating them, we offer hospitality to the person who caries shame in a secret when we are open to hear their confession. When we truly welcome the speaker by hearing the words spoken, the meanings behind, underneath, and even *concealed* within the words are received. When what is spoken has deep importance to the speaker, being heard is like being warmly welcomed after a long, lonely, and difficult journey—truly the Prodigal Son's experience.

We are a bridge for others to be able to receive and accept God's grace and love when we carry a clear awareness of the boundless love of God for ourselves and for others. When previously anticipated judgment does not materialize, secret keepers become enabled to break their silence and reach for the newly anticipated acceptance and hope for the future. We are reminded of the women in Pastor Dan's church who shared their secrets. *Ministry is not entirely in what we do but, more importantly, it lies in the character of how we are—our being, as much as in our doing.* When we convey to people the kind of welcoming grace we see in the father of the Prodigal Son, they are more likely to be able to speak of whatever they carry with shame. In contrast, David's "welcome" of Absalom— even though with a kiss—does not convey acceptance and grace. It says that Absalom is not completely received. Absalom knows this.

The importance of being heard and what it means to the one speaking varies with the importance of the message. When we realize that the speaker is telling a painful secret that was, in some cases, hidden over many years' time and carried with painful feelings of shame, anger, loss, and fear, we must realize that the importance of being heard is at its highest level. Our hearing also must include acceptance of the speaker and the secret.

Our challenge is to overcome our disbelief in the generosity of God's grace, so that we will be able to convey the reality of Jesus' words in our ministries with those who carry excessive shame in secrets they cannot bear and cannot share.

Telling Means Healing

Healing begins for the person who has a painful secret when the secret is finally told. The person keeping a shameful secret may have spent years going over and over, reviewing and obsessing over the source of the secret and not being able to move closer to healing. One man, who, as a child, had been abused by a priest, had kept his silence for many years. Although the church had given his family a settlement for their silence, he finally broke that agreement and his silence. After he revealed his secret, he said that it wasn't until he spoke out that he began to heal. After many years of keeping the painful and shameful secret, telling the secret is what began his healing process. Telling is both an end and a beginning. It is the end of carrying the secret one-self, and it is the beginning of the process of healing. Telling the secret empowers the secret teller. The burden of the secret is no longer carried alone. The isolation of holding and hiding a secret alone is defeated when someone hears the secret. The secret keeper feels like a part of the community again.

This man was not enabled to tell by a welcoming presence, nor did he tell it as a confession. Instead he, like numbers of others, got to the point where he was not able to contain the secret any longer. He needed a new life for himself. This is one of the ways in which people arrive at their telling. Many others cannot get to this point without some recognition of the possibility of a receptive presence. This man became one among those who opened the way for many others with similar experiences to tell their secrets.

After telling, the healing can continue internally as secret tellers continue to put pieces together and move beyond their hiding. Healing depends on having someone to talk with about the secret over a period of time and may include forgiveness of one's self or of others. Some-times this is not possible, and forgiving should not be at the top of our agenda as action necessary for the secret keeper to heal. Forgiving self or others is a choice the secret keeper makes. Our role is helping secret keepers see the value in forgiveness, without our trying to sell them on it. When we place excessive emphasis on forgiving, the secret keeper is likely to experience more shame for not being able to forgive.

Those who have kept secrets have other important choices to make. Their kept secrets have had places in their lives and roles in shaping how they have lived and believed. There is an opportunity, after tell-ing, for secret keepers to make new choices about life. Their lives no longer have to be shaped by the secret. In a sense, they get to choose a new measure of freedom. They also have other choices to make, for example, deciding who else should hear the secret and who should not. There are also choices they may be forced to make because they have told the secret. These choices may have played a role in their struggle with deciding whether to tell.

Keeping the Secret You Hear

Even though keeping what we have heard in confidence was dealt with earlier in chapter 2, this is a point at which we should be reminded that this role of keeping the secrets is part of the process of hearing secrets. We are trusted and must be faithful in our receiving and keeping what we are told. Listening does not end when the speaker stops talking.

After the secret is told, it has the potential of being seen as a blessing. The secret told and retold in confidence may enable both the hearer and the secret keeper to recognize the blessing and grace it has carried. We see the dynamic of the blessing and grace that can be discovered as we explore the story of Joseph.

Part III: Secret Becoming Blessing

The story of Joseph, son of Jacob and Rachel,[18] provides an account of the transformation that can come when a secret is revealed (Genesis 37–50). As a young man, Joseph was his father's favorite. This fact was painfully obvious to his brothers. Joseph further annoyed his brothers with his dream and its interpretation that he reported to his brothers, symbolizing them bowing down to him. That future was hard for his older brothers to swallow.

While they were out tending their father's sheep, the brothers saw an opportunity to get rid of him. They first conspired to kill Joseph and throw him into a pit. Brother Reuben interceded and persuaded them just to throw him in the pit but not kill him (Reuben's plan being to rescue him later). They threw him into a pit with the intention of leaving him there, but some traders came by and the brothers, realizing they could also make some money, sold Joseph to them—returning home with his special robe soiled with blood from a slaughtered goat. They lied to their father, saying that a wild animal had killed Joseph. The secret began to cause pain in the family as Jacob mourned the death of his son. The brothers, although free from their annoying and, to them, arrogant brother, were then trapped in the dynamics of keeping the secret. It would play a role in their lives for many years.

The traders sold Joseph to Pharaoh's captain of the guard, Potiphar. Joseph prospered in Potiphar's house until Potiphar's wife falsely accused him of trying to rape her. To make matters worse, Joseph was thrown into prison where, strangely, he continued to prosper—signified by all the prisoners being put in Joseph's care.

Joseph's gift of dream interpretation brought him into a powerful position in Pharaoh's court when he rightly interpreted dreams of two prisoners who were in his care. Pharaoh learned of Joseph's gift when he had a dream others could not interpret and he heard about Joseph's gift from one of those prisoners. Joseph carefully gave God the credit for being the source of his interpretations, and then he informed Pharaoh that the dreams he described symbolized seven years of plenty that would be followed by seven years of famine. He recommended ways for the Egyptians not only to be able to survive but also to thrive through the coming plight. Pharaoh was pleased with Joseph's plans and appointed him second in command in all of Egypt, with the authority to put his plans into action. We see how effective Joseph's plan was when we read that during the famine "Every country came to Egypt to buy grain from Joseph" (Genesis 41:57).

Back home, Jacob's family also suffered from the drought, but they learned that Egypt had grain. He sent his sons (except for Benjamin—the youngest, born to Rachel) to Egypt to buy grain so they could survive. When they arrived, they met Joseph, their long-lost brother. While Joseph knew who *they* were, they did not recognize him even when he inquired about their father and asked about whether they had any other brothers. He provided them with the grain they needed and sent them back with the money they brought placed back in their bags of grain. He also warned them that they could not see him again if they did not return with their youngest brother.

When Jacob's food supplies were again depleted, the brothers planned a return to Egypt, but with great anxiety about bringing Benjamin with them. It certainly was not what their father wanted them to do. They saw no way out. They believed that Joseph would not receive them without Benjamin. To persuade Jacob to let Benjamin go with them, Judah promised that he would offer himself as a substitute should any ill befall Benjamin.

They returned to Egypt with Benjamin. After some family drama, including Joseph having to excuse himself to go weep privately when he was twice overcome with emotion. Finally, Joseph confessed to them that he was their brother. He followed this up with a demonstration of overwhelming hospitality, welcoming his whole family and all their flocks to come to Egypt and dwell on prime real estate offered by the Pharaoh. The support and cooperation of the Pharaoh in the hospitality offered to Jacob's family revealed the depth of respect and appreciation with which Joseph was held.

Where his brothers were certain he should be resentful and angry with them and wish to do them harm, this was not what they got. The brothers who sold him into slavery received a warm welcome—an act of redemption for the whole family. Joseph explained, "Now, don't be upset and don't be angry with yourselves that you sold me here. . . . God sent me before you to make sure you'd survive and to rescue your lives in this amazing way. You didn't send me here; it was God" (45:5, 7). Joseph's response demonstrated the impact the grace of God could have on situations of divisive and destructive secrets.

The secret Joseph's brothers had kept for many years turned into a blessing when Joseph revealed himself. What we see in the person of Joseph, as he does this, is an ability to let go of any resentment he could justifiably hold. He did not dwell on the great wrong done to him. Instead, he said, full of grace and awareness of how God is, that God was able to work with what his brothers did and bring out of it good for all. The outcome of the revealing of the secret was truly full of God's grace and hope, full of potential and the reality of forgiveness, reconciliation, and restoration. How easily it could have been quite different.

Conclusion

Let me call something to your attention. We looked briefly at the cultural context that was the setting for Jesus telling the story of the

Prodigal Son. The father's behavior in welcoming his son home was so far out of the cultural bounds of the day that we should factor this reality into our reading of the story. What was Jesus doing? I would answer "the usual." As usual, he was dynamically confronting the people to whom he spoke. "Look at this. See this father who is one of you. He knows the rules and the expectations of his role as a father in relation to his sons. He knows the powerful value of honor and dignity—his standing within the community. And he ignores all of this, acting like a fool—first, as he handed his son his inheritance when he asked for it, and then, as he welcomed that despicable son back into the family, as an honored member. Then he even dropped all of his respectability and ran down the street to greet this son and see him safely back home."

The message of Jesus goes further. The *older* son also was disrespectful, but in a different way—refusing to attend the party his father threw for the found brother. The father gave this very same elder son comparable respect, love, and honor. What is wrong with this father? He threw away everything that his community respected in how he behaved in his relationship with these two cheeky sons. Instead of being bound by what was expected culturally, he went somewhere else for the respect and love he called forth to relate to both sons. That image Jesus gives us is what we have available to us today and tomorrow. God breaks the rules of expectation *we* have for God every time we turn around. Just like Jesus told us. What a message for the shame-bound secret keeper who has the possibility to confess!

The father in this parable represents God. But the father's behavior is not what the people who heard Jesus' story anticipated. The father did not meet the expectations of the community. He threw away all of his dignity and honor in the process of demonstrating the depth of his love for both of his sons. What does this mean for us today as ministers to people who are burdened with shameful secrets and want a place to lay them down and still be safe? Can we believe this image of God as the gracious one who is willing to be vulnerable and who welcomes and receives us *and* the secret keeper—regardless?

In spite of the powerful message we find in this parable, we resist accepting the incredible depth of the grace of God. It is as difficult for us to accept as it was for the people to whom Jesus spoke. If we can accept it as showing us who God is, then we would experience what Emil Brunner described, "Were we really to grasp it with all our heart, our life would overflow with joy and love."[19]

We have to run counter to cultural expectations in order to fulfill who we are called to be as we respond to the confessions of secrets. It is hard for us to run counter to cultural expectations because doing so is right where we find the source of our shame—right in the midst of cultural expectations. We are vulnerable. In the cultural context of the parable, Jesus said something that was inestimably outrageous as he painted the picture of the father for those listening. Just like the father he described, Jesus, in telling this story, was running counter to cultural expectations. His words continue to be countercultural—no matter how much we try to make his words conform to what we expect.

The story of Joseph being so badly treated by his jealous brothers and becoming a secret kept by his brothers for many years should not have turned out the way it did. He was gone from his family, and even though he became unrecognizable by them, he was in the end able to bring the blessing of life to them along with restoration within the family. Within Joseph's experience of harm intended by his brothers was a presence of grace available to him for his future and for the future of his family and for the entire people of Israel. Frederick Buechner captures the reality of this presence of grace when he says, "I learned something about how even tragedy can be a means of grace that I might never have come to any other way."[20] Joseph was able to manifest this grace-filled presence to his family. Joseph could have made the choice not to confront his brothers with the secret they had kept. His maintaining, with them, the silence they had kept for years would have closed out the possibility for restoration and reconciliation.

When their father is dead, Joseph's brothers resurrect their fear that Joseph still carries resentment toward them. They offer themselves to be his slaves, but Joseph clearly responds, "Don't be afraid. Am I God? You planned something bad for me, but God produced something good from it, in order to save the lives of many people, just as he's doing today" (50:19-20). Grace was present from the beginning, even in the midst of the treachery Joseph's brothers perpetrated. It was present as possibility that a positive future could be made from the destructive experience Joseph's brothers imposed on his life.

Careful listeners open the possibility for peace in the secret keeper's life through their listening and demonstration of the presence of God's grace and love. When we are able to hear a painful secret, we give a gift of great value to the person who has held the secret. We bring them into awareness of God's boundless love that they can realize is for them, just as they have been—just as they are—even with their secret exposed.

Workshop 1

Secrecy in Our Midst

Bible Study (Mark 5:24b-34)

Introduction: We miss a great deal when we read scripture, especially when the stories are familiar to us. Our analytic powers are turned down and we read at face value and through our traditional and cultural lenses, not allowing ourselves to make discoveries. Other scriptures may become barriers to truly receiving some secrets because we know there are scriptures that will condemn the secret teller. How can we be a truly hospitable listener? I encourage participants to be open as they read and interpret scripture, always keeping in mind the person and spirit of Jesus whose judgment of others was basically limited to those who abused their power. Check out your own judgments with Jesus. If we allow our judgments to prevail we shut off the valuable grace that could come through our receiving the confession.

Here maybe we can do some discovery in relation to hearing shameful secrets.

Beginning Prayer: Pray for openness to hear God's word for us in the scripture we will be exploring. We ask for help to discover what we need to learn about our ministry.

The Scripture Narrative: Jesus is on his way to heal a young woman at the request of her father, Jairus, who is one of the leaders of the synagogue. A crowd surrounds Jesus as he proceeds. A woman who has been bleeding for twelve years and has tried unsuccessfully to be cured by every physician has told herself that if she can just touch Jesus' garment, she will be healed. Because she is bleeding, she is seen as unclean. How can she reach him? It is a big crowd, and she is unclean and should not touch *anyone*—let alone Jesus. She manages to touch his cloak (Luke 8:44 and Matthew 9:20 say "the fringe" or "hem" of his clothes/cloak). She must have been crawling to reach him, because people who would recognize her from the community would be avoiding her and calling out "unclean!" if they saw her.

She immediately knows she has been healed. Jesus, with the crowd pressing around him, asks who touched his clothes. I suspect the disciples laughed at this as they said, "Don't you see the crowd pressing against you? Yet you ask, 'Who touched me?' " (Mark 5:31). Jesus was reacting to the feeling of power flowing from him because of someone's *significant* touch. He knows he has been the conduit of grace. The woman admits it was she (confesses), and Jesus proclaims she is healed by her faith.

Invitation to Act Out the Scene: Pretending to be part of the scripture story is a way to get to the heart of what we may miss. For example, imagine being this woman who has been unclean for so long, trying to get through a crowd unnoticed. How convinced she must have been that now she could be healed! The others in the crowd are so focused on Jesus they do not notice her—until he calls attention to her.

Jesus' Circumstances: He is on his way to heal the daughter of Jarius, a leader of the synagogue. Jesus is known to be unclean from the touch of the woman. Why didn't he just let her be healed and not call attention to it? Then no one would know he had been made unclean. What we can see is that Jesus was willing to be *vulnerable in his reception of this "daughter."* Jesus was also a *conduit* for the power that healed her. He did not take any action himself until he proclaimed what had already taken place. "At that very moment, Jesus recognized that power had gone out from him" (v. 30).

Jesus Teaches Us to Respond: First we see that Jesus is willing to be vulnerable by reaching out to this woman who is not only ill but also filled with shame. Then he teaches us two responses we can make: "I see you" and "I see your faith." The woman expressed her faith in her efforts to reach Jesus (her last resort?). Somehow she had the ability to see that there was still some hope beyond her current circumstances and grace existing in the situation—both of which Jesus pronounces when he affirms the healing she has already experienced.

Discussion: How can this scripture help us in efforts to listen to confessions by secret keepers? Are there ways in which your eyes were opened by seeing this story anew?

Closing with Prayer: Pray in thanksgiving for the ways in which God meets us in the midst of our lives. Pray that we may be receptive to see the surprises offered.

Workshop 2

What Do *You* Want to Avoid?

Getting Ready to Hear Confessions: Self-awareness is a necessity. But here is an assurance: We know we can't be prepared to hear everything that people might be holding as shameful secrets, but we can examine ourselves to be aware of those issues we are not able to listen to or speak about. When you identify something you want to avoid that might be a secret keeper's issue, you can make a plan for how you might be able to change and become ready to face what you may now want to avoid.

Self-Awareness in Preparing to Listen: When we listen to others' confessions we need to remain very aware of how we are reacting inside and out. This is necessary even while we must keep the person speaking at the center of our focus. You can do that. It may sound contradictory, but you can. It is a bit like driving a car when you have to remain aware of what is in front of you, what is behind you, who is passing you, what the road surface conditions are, and on and on. We do many things at once. Our ability to focus on the person speaking hinges on our being willing to go with them into the area in which they are sharing. When it repels us, we turn to our self and avoid their issue. Then we do not hear what they are saying. There is no redemption, no grace received, no welcome with hospitality for them.

Prayer in Being Prepared: Being centered and willing to be vulnerable makes it possible for us to become conduits of the grace of God to those who tell their secrets. We use prayer to ask for these blessings of being open to the Holy Spirit and the vulnerability that requires of us.

Invitation: Planning to Be Ready: In a small group, work together on the areas in which you need to change or grow. Here are some guiding questions:

- What do you *know* you want to avoid? You might want to share what you think makes this a difficult area for you.

- What does your faith (theology) say about this issue? This is an opportunity to reflect on your theology and let it address the issue you want to avoid. Does your avoidance have any roots in your faith?

- What research could you do that would help with your comfort level? Sometimes we are uneasy when we feel we are not informed.

- With whom could you have conversations to help you feel comfortable with this area/topic/issue? Discussion with someone who is familiar with the issue you want to avoid is a great resource for growth in comfort.

Decisions and Commitments: Commitments can relate to your preparation choices and directions and also include your willingness to reconsider where you are now with some issue(s). These considerations may also have an impact on your theology/faith. You may begin to see issues through the eyes of faith that you may have left as separate from your faith until this time. Share commitments and resources with others in the group, and give feedback to one another.

Closing with Prayer: Give thanks that we may be able to welcome growth and insight and that we may be patient with ourselves and with one another.

Preparing for After-Care for Those Who Reveal Secrets

When Someone Has Told: Recall Margaret from chapter 5. We met Margaret as she talked with her pastor about her struggle deciding whether to tell her long-kept secret. Her story was left unfinished. She had not decided. The pastor (rightly) had not told her what to do. Margaret expressed her concerns about how others might feel about her if they heard her secret. Now *we* are going to be members of the same congregation where Margaret has been a faithful member and leader for many years.

Participation: Review Margaret's story together. She has decided to reveal her secret to friends within the congregation. We will use her story to think through our responses to someone who tells their secret. I have specified Margaret here, but these are applicable to anyone who has told his or her secret.

- Prepare yourself for care with Margaret by *praying* for support, understanding, and openness so that you might be a conduit of grace for Margaret.

- Be clear with yourself, through *self-awareness*, about how you feel about Margaret *with her secret.*

- Be prepared to *reaffirm* Margaret.

- Be *available*—make yourself present to Margaret.

- *Raise the issue* of her secret with her at appropriate times. Do so tentatively and not with pressure or undue expectation. This is a way to tell her you are available to hear more.

- Be *aware* if Margaret stops being active in the church, and reach out. Her shame may be taking control, and she is trying to hide.

- *Recognize* when you are in over your head and need to call to make a referral to another professional for her care.

- *Notice* if she wants to go over and over the secret and it is too much for you.

- There may be times to *offer spiritual care* by praying with Margaret or talking with her about faith issues related to her secret.

Discussion: Talk together about what you discovered in this exercise and what might need to be added to this understanding of "after-care" for use in the church. What do you wonder about as we have done this work?

Closing with Prayer: This might be an opportunity to think both about the prayer you need for yourself as you listen and respond to Margaret over time and the prayer you might offer for her and her renewal.

Workshop 4

NOTE: Before beginning with this workshop note that there are two alternatives offered. Participants can decide which they want to pursue, so read over both before beginning.

Alternative 1: Responding to Denise

Denise's Story: This story could be one a minister hears from a parishioner or from someone from the surrounding community. It is, sadly, not a rare story. While not the sole subject of shameful secrets, it could be the most common of secrets—sexual abuse of a child. We hear Denise's story in two parts. We will have **someone play the role of Denise** and read her words. The words of **the minister to whom** she speaks are not provided and will be left up to the persons who play that role. We will hear the first part of Denise's story and then discuss the minister's response, including how she or he feels about that response. We will also hear how Denise feels about how she and her secret were received. Then we will do the second part of her story. There could be a new person reading for Denise in the second part as well as a new person being pastor to her.

As Denise speaks, she should stop where there are breaks and try to feel what the pace is for the rest. The idea is to give the minister/

listener an opportunity to respond, but it is up to the listener to respond or not. Remember, Denise has never said this before.

There is not one correct response to what Denise says. Many responses can be helpful, but not all. Less helpful responses offer opportunities for discussion. I encourage those who are the minister to **avoid both interpreting and asking questions.**

Those Who Are Observing: Keep notes on what your reactions are when Denise speaks. How do you feel? Where does your mind go? What do you *want* to say?

Denise has asked if she could talk with you—something is troubling her.

Denise Speaks: "Hear My Story"

"I am sitting on a towel on my mother's lap. We are in the car. My dad is driving. My mother is distraught. We are on our way to the hospital. The time of day is unclear. It seems like it is dark or dusk. This is the only clear memory I have about this incident."

"The story I was told, but do not remember, is that we—my brother and I—were playing on the 'slide' my father made from a single waxed board. I remember the slide and its set up. It leaned against the roof of our playhouse. There must have been a ladder to get to the top of the slide."

"I have an old photo. I can see it in my mind. My brother and I are sitting on the slide. I understand that the photo was taken before I slipped off the side of the slide—my virginity lost on the edge of the board."

"I know this because my mother told me this part on the eve of my wedding. Even as I say this, I can't believe she did this. She told me then so I could explain to my husband why I was not a virgin. Of course she never told me this before—and I was angry about that when she told me. I was angry because I knew she didn't tell me because she believed that thinking I was a virgin would be the only thing that would keep me from having sex before I got married! I was surprised. Was this how my mother saw me?"

"In the many years since, I have never told anyone about this experience—other than my husband and I do not *remember* telling him. There did not seem to be an issue about this on our wedding night."

Those Who Are Observing: Keep notes on what your reactions are when Denise speaks. How do you feel? Where does your mind go? What do you *want* to say?

Reflections: What are your feelings and reactions? From "Denise"? From the minister? From others? Would a minister ever hear anything like this story?

Denise Speaks Again: (meeting with the minister at another time)

"What I said before is all I know from that childhood experience. But I think the story goes on—maybe it's strange—but I think it's connected. You know I was married, but it didn't last too long. I remember finding reasons not to go to bed when my husband did. Sometimes what I did was sit on the side of the bed and cry. I didn't know why."

"We got divorced, but before that—when we were separated— before the divorce, I started hooking up with men. I don't know how many. I started to keep a list—but there were some whose names I don't think I ever knew."

"That was when I remembered the ride in the car with my mother so upset—and my cousin."

"He was a lot older than I was. He might have even been twenty and I was just six or seven."

"I don't believe the story about the slide—it seems impossible"

Reflections: What are your feelings and reactions? From "Denise"? From the minister? From others? Would a minister ever hear anything like this story?

Praying for Denise: Be intentional about what you would want to pray for as you pray for Denise. Where would you focus? What gifts do you want for her?

Closing with Prayer: This could be a prayer for Denise or for those who hear her story that they can be present to her in her pain and confusion.

Alternative 2: *Secrets and Lies*

The Process: This alternative requires that the leader locate the film *Secrets and Lies* and all participants view it together. Participants might begin with a brief general discussion of the movie before responding to the questions offered here. This discussion could begin simply with the question, "What did you see?"

Holding in mind the understandings about keeping secrets and confessing them and the theological foundations offered in this book, reflect on the following:

All of the characters in the movie are struggling as we meet them:

- Cynthia is depressed.

- Roxanne is angry.

- Maurice is frustrated.

- Monica feels like a failure.

- Hortense has just lost all the family she has known.

(Of course, these are snapshots and do not give us the whole picture of any of the characters.)

Offering Care for the Characters: Choose one character to begin with and imagine—maybe write some notes—what if she or he had gone to talk with her or his minister? Participants could go through the whole cast of characters asking this question. What would have happened? How would you have helped each of them? What difference could these conversations have made in their lives? I would also recommend seeing Monica and Maurice together and Cynthia and Roxanne together, to work on their relationships with one another. Role playing these meetings would be helpful.

Participants might consider creating a prayer for each meeting. Without knowing what was underneath their outward behavior and feelings expressed, what would you pray for or about?

Notes

Introduction

1. I recognize that some people hold secrets that they do not feel they need or want to tell. This work does not focus on these people. I have no intention to depict such people as having a problem because they do not want to tell. Nor do I want to encourage others to see people who do not need or do not choose to tell secrets as being wrong.

2. The most recent volume published by Warren is *PostSecret: Confessions on Life, Death and God* (New York: Harper/Collins, 2009). Others include *PostSecret, My Secret, The Secret Lives of Men and Women,* and *A Lifetime of Secrets.*

3. Frank Warren, *A Lifetime of Secrets* (New York: Harper/Collins, 2009), introduction.

4. Frank Warren, *PostSecret: Confessions on Life, Death, and God* (New York: HarperCollins, 2009), ix.

5. Paul Tournier, *Secrets* (Atlanta: John Knox Press, 1977), 9.

6. Harriet G. Lerner, *The Dance of Deception: Pretending and Truth Telling in Women's Lives* (New York: Harper Perennial, 1993), 39.

7. It is common for family members who hear a family secret for the first time to have this experience of relief and of having somehow "known." In the earlier story, Josie told of having this experience of "knowing."

1. Hearing Confessions

1. David Hogue, *Remembering the Future/Imagining the Past: Story, Ritual, and the Human Brain* (Cleveland, Ohio: Pilgrim Press, 2003), 165.

2. Daniel L. Schacter, *The Seven Sins of Memory: How the Mind Forgets and Remembers* (New York: Houghton Mifflin, 2001), 171.

3. Ronald W. Richardson, *Creating a Healthier Church: Family Systems Theory, Leadership, and Congregational Life* (Minneapolis: Fortress Press, 1996), 175.

4. Pastor Dan used a statistic current at the time he preached this sermon. Those statistics reported that domestic abuse in the United States occurred every 12 to 15 seconds. More recent statistics tell us that "between 600,000 and six million women are victims of domestic violence each year." From Domestic Violence Resource Center, "Domestic Violence Statistics," accessed September 3, 2013, http://dvrc-or.org/domestic/violence/resources/C61/.

5. See Sara Jenkins, *Past Present: Recording Life Stories of Older People* (Washington. D. C.: St. Alban's Parish, 1978). Richard L. Morgan, *Remembering Your Story: Creating Your Own Spiritual Autobiography* (Nashville: Upper Room, 2002).

6. These questions could effectively be converted into requests like, "Tell me about your greatest accomplishment in your life."

7. The story of Abraham welcoming the strangers in the desert, found in Genesis 18, provides the image used here. See also my book *Hearing beyond the Words: How to Become a Listening Pastor* (Nashville: Abingdon, 2006).

8. Michael P. Nichols, *The Lost Art of Listening* (New York: Guilford Press, 1995).

9. Limitations to this promise will be discussed in chapter 2.

2. Listening Is Not Trading Secrets

1. This story is told in *Hearing beyond the Words* (Nashville: Abingdon Press, 2006), 35–37. I repeat it briefly here because it makes the point so clearly.

2. For example, the United Church of Christ has very clear and usable guidance on its website, ucc.org. Seventh-Day Adventists provide a thorough *Minister's Handbook* inclusive of ethical and boundary issues.

3. An experienced pastor reflected to me the struggle he had and the seriousness with which he took confidentiality in prayer requests. He knew he had to keep clarity about who did not want prayer requests or their identity made public.

4. Karen Lebacqz and Joseph D. Driskill, *Ethics and Spiritual Care: A Guide for Pastors, Chaplains and Spiritual Directors* (Nashville: Abingdon, 2000), 37.

5. Ibid., 55.

6. See: Ronald W. Richardson, *Creating a Healthier Church: Family Systems Theory, Leadership and Congregational Life* (Minneapolis: Fortress Press, 1996), 173–80.

7. I am not suggesting that the weekly meals were the only factor in the growth of the church but that the story illustrates the carrying of hope for others.

8. Lebacqz and Driskill, 52.

9. Pamela Cooper-White, *The Cry of Tamar: Violence against Women and the Church's Response* (Minneapolis: Fortress, 1995). See especially "Clergy Sexual Abuse," 126–44. See also Cooper-Whit's article, "Soul Stealing: Power Relations in Pastoral Sexual Abuse," *The Christian Century*, February 20, 1991.

10. See Nancy Werking Poling, *Victim to Survivor: Women Recovering from Clergy Sexual Abuse* (Cleveland: United Church Press, 1999). Poling emphasizes the role of secrecy in the perpetuation of clergy abuse. See xiii.

11. "Clergy Sexual Misconduct: Awareness and Prevention." Baylor University. Waco Texas, 2009.

3. The Pastor as the Bearer of Secrets

1. I have used the image of male pastors and their wives to make this point because it has been a practice for some pastors to share with their spouses the burdens they carry, more so than it has been for male spouses to carry their wives' burdens. Maybe this has more to do with the limited numbers of male ministry spouses historically.

2. See stephenministries.org. Over 11,000 congregations and 500,000 trained caregivers have been part of Stephen Ministries.

3. G. Lloyd Rediger, *Clergy Killers: Guidance for Pastors and Congregations Under Attack* (Louisville: Westminster John Knox, 1997), 198.

4. Here are examples of helpful internet resources regarding counseling credentialing and licensing: The American Psychological Association (APA), http://www.apa.org; National Association of Social Workers, http://www.socialworkers.org; American Association for Marriage and Family Therapy (AAMFT), http://www.aamft.org; American Counseling Association, http://counseling.org. The American Association of Pastoral Counselors provides a very helpful site: http://www.aapc.org.

4. Is What You Hear the Truth?

1. See Exodus 2 and 3 for this part of Moses's story.

2. Paul Ekman, *Why Kids Lie: How Parents Can Encourage Truthfulness* (New York: Charles Scribner's Sons, 1989), 6.

3. In his little book *Secrets,* Paul Tournier tells a delightful story about a little girl called Frances and how she *surprises herself* by telling her mother a totally unnecessary lie. He makes a point about becoming an individual involving separating from parents and the role deception plays in this process, (Richmond: John Knox Press, 1965), 7–8.

4. Vickie Lewis, *Side-by-Side: A Photographic History of American Women in War* (New York: Stewart. Tabori & Chang, 1999), 24.

5. The movie *Schindler's List* may be the most familiar story of the efforts and risks involved and the deceptions perpetrated to save the lives of Jews. Irena Sendler is a lesser-known hero from the Holocaust. She worked for the Germans as a plumbing and sewer specialist in Warsaw and, on the side, smuggled infants out of the ghetto in the bottom of her toolbox and used a burlap sack to conceal older children whom she rescued. She rescued 2,500 children with her deceptions. For further information about Irena Sendler see: "Life in a Jar: The Irena Sendler Project," 2006, accessed October 20, 2012, http://www.irenasendler.com; PBS, "Irena Sendler: In the Name of their Mothers," Public Broadcasting Service, May, 2011, accessed October 20, 2012, http://www.pbs.org/programs/irena-sendler; and Yitta Halberstam and Judith Leventhal, *Small Miracles of the Holocaust,* The Lyons Press, 1st ed. (August 13 2008).

6. Diane M. Komp. *Anatomy of a Lie: The Truth about Lies and Why Good People Tell Them* (Grand Rapids: Zondervan, 1998).

7. Bill Hybels, *Transparency: Discovering the Rewards of Truth-Telling* (Grand Rapids: Zondervan, 1997), 72.

8. Ibid., 73.

5. Can Shame Release the Truth?

1. Harold Ivan Smith, *A Long Shadowed Grief: Suicide and Its Aftermath* (Cambridge, Massachusetts: Cowley Publications, 2006).

2. Erik H. Erikson. *Identity: Youth and Crisis* (New York: Norton, 1968), 107–14.

3. John S. Mbiti, *African Religions and Philosophy* (Garden City, New York: Doubleday, 1970), 141.

4. Children with secrets of sexual abuse may succeed at being "perfect."

6. How Memory Helps, Defends, and Distorts

1. David Hogue, *Remembering the Future/Imagining the Past: Story, Ritual and the Human Brain* (Cleveland: Pilgrim Press, 2003), 27.

2. Miroslav Volf, *The End of Memory: Remembering Rightly in a Violent World* (Grand Rapids: Eerdmans, 2006), 97.

3. Hogue, 79.

4. Ibid., 76.

5. Ibid.

6. Ibid., 68.

7. Jean Beaven Abernethy, *Old Is Not a Four-Letter Word* (Nashville: Abingdon, 1975), 22.

8. Hogue, 27.

9. Ibid., 68.

10. Daniel L. Schacter, *The Seven Sins of Memory: How the Mind Forgets and Remembers* (New York: Houghton Mifflin, 2001), 34–35.

11. Hogue, 72.

12. Volf, 11–13.

13. Hogue, 173.

14. Schacter, 23–27.

15. Ibid., 7.

16. Schacter, 9.

17. Hogue, 60.

18. Ibid., 61.

19. Ibid., 172.

20. Ibid., 71.

21. Volf, 93.

22. Schacter, 3.

23. Hogue, 74.

24. Schacter, 84.

25. Volf, 47–48.

26. See Tom Rutherford, "Reunited," Guideposts (January 2000): 30–34.

27. Hogue, 70.

28. Ibid., 67.

29. Ibid., 5.

30. Alexander McCall Smith. *The No.1 Ladies' Detective Agency* (New York: Anchor Books, 2002), 15.

7. From Generation to Generation

1. Candace R. Benyei, *Understanding Clergy Misconduct in Religious Systems* (New York: Haworth Press, 1998), 104.

2. A. A. Anderson, "David, Bathsheba, and Uriah," *Word Biblical Commentary, 11, 2 Samuel* (Dallas, Texas: Word Books, 1989), 156.

3. Tony W. Cartledge, *Smyth & Helwys Bible Commentary 1 & 2 Samuel* (Macon, Georgia: Smyth & Helwys, 2001), 505. Cartledge offers this literal translation, "Do not let this thing be evil in your eyes."

4. Benyei, xiii–xiv.

5. Bruce C. Birch, "1 & 2 Samuel." *The New Interpreter's Bible*, vol. 2 (Nashville: Abingdon, 1998), 1304. The act is rape.

6. Phyllis Trible, *Texts of Terror: Literary-Feminist Readings of Biblical Narratives* (Philadelphia, Pennsylvania: Fortress, 1984), 48.

7. This is a repeat of what David said to Joab about the death of Uriah, "Do not let this thing be evil in your eyes."

8. Trible, 52. The word used for "desolate" is used elsewhere to mean destroyed by an enemy (Lamentations 1:16) or torn to pieces by an animal (Lamentations 3:11).

9. Cartledge, 539. Tamar would no longer be welcome to live with her other unmarried, princess sisters in the King's household because she was raped, no longer a virgin. Heather A. McKay adds to the meaning of Tamar's situation referring to it as "abuse that effectively eliminated her from marriage and a woman's recognized future." "Lying and Deceit in Families: The Duping of Isaac and Tamar" Patricia Dutcher-Walls, *The Family in Life and Death: The Family in Ancient Israel Sociological and Archaeological Perspectives* (New York: T&T Clark, 2009), 40.

10. Birch, 1305.

11. Ibid., 1309.

12. Ibid., 1309–10.

13. Trible, 55.

14. Walter Brueggemann, "First and Second Samuel," *Interpretation: A Bible Commentary for Teaching and Preaching* (Louisville: John Knox Press, 1990), 293.

15. Birch, 1316.

16. Ibid.

17. These stories do not stand alone in scripture as stories the church does not often face. Genesis 19 and Judges 19 offer painful stories many Christians do not even know exist in scripture.

18. Benyei, 107.

19. Ibid., 105.

20. Louise Penny, *A Trick of the Light* (New York: Minotaur, 2011), 11.

21. Benyei, 109.

22. Ibid., 121.

23. Birch, 1316.

8. Hearing Secrets as a Means of Grace

1. Kenneth Bailey, "Jacob and the Prodigal Son: A New Identity Story," *Theological Review,* XVIII/1 (April 1997): 69.

2. Joel W. Huffstetler, *Boundless Love: The Parable of the Prodigal Son and Reconciliation* (Lanham, Maryland: University Press of America, 2008), 3.

3. Alicia Batten, "Dishonour, Gender and the Parable of the Prodigal Son," *Toronto Journal of Theology*, 13/2 (Fall 1997): 194.

4. Bernard Brandon Scott, *Hear Then the Parable: A Commentary on the Parables of Jesus* (Minneapolis: Fortress Press, 1989), 116.

5. Joachim Jeremias, *Rediscovering the Parables* (New York: Charles Scribner's Sons, 1966), 102.

6. Bruce J. Malina and Richard L. Rohrbaugh, *Social-Science Commentary on the Synoptic Gospels* (Minneapolis: Fortress Press, 1992), 372.

7. Batten, 194.

8. Malina and Rohrbaugh, 372.

9. Kenneth E. Bailey, *The Cross and the Prodigal Son: Luke 15 through the Eyes of Middle Eastern Peasants,* 2nd ed. (Downers Grove, IL: InterVarsity Press, 2005), 67

10. Ibid., 66–67.

11. Huffstetler, 29.

12. Cartledge, 554.

13. Ibid.

14. Huffstetler,16.

15. Jeremy Punt, "The Prodigal Son and the Blade Runner," *Journal of Theology for Southern Africa*, 128 (July 2007): 98.

16. Bailey, 68.

17. Emil Brunner, *Sowing and Reaping: The Parables of Jesus*, trans. Thomas Wieser (Richmond: John Knox Press, 1946), 39.

18. Genesis 30 gives us the story of Jacob and Rachel's long wait to bear a son together, and Joseph becomes beloved because Rachel is his mother. The only other son born to Rachel was Benjamin. She died in childbirth with him (Genesis 35:16-21).

19. Ibid., Brunner.

20. Frederick Buechner, *Telling Secrets: A Memoir* (San Francisco: Harper, 1991), 32.

Bibliography

Abernethy, Jean Beaven, *Old Is Not a Four-Letter Word*. Nashville: Abingdon, 1975.

Anderson, A. A. "David, Bathsheba and Uriah," *Word Biblical Commentary, 11, 2 Samuel*. Dallas: Word Books, 1989.

Bailey, Kenneth E., "Jacob and the Prodigal Son: A New Identity Story," *Theological Review*, XVIII/1. April 1997.

————. *The Cross and the Prodigal Son: Luke 15 through the Eyes of Middle Eastern Peasants*, 2n ed. Downers Grove, Illinois: Inter-Varsity Press, 2005.

Batten, Alicia. "Dishonour, Gender and the Parable of the Prodigal Son," *Toronto Journal of Theology*, 13/2, Fall 1997.

Benyei, Candace R. *Understanding Clergy Misconduct in Religious Systems: Scapegoating, Family Secrets, and the Abuse of Power*. New York: Haworth Press, 1998.

Birch, Bruce C. "1 & 2 Samuel," *The New Interpreter's Bible*, vol. 2. Nashville: Abingdon, 1998.

Brueggemann, Walter. "First and Second Samuel," *Interpretation: A Bible Commentary for Teaching and Preaching*. Louisville: John Knox Press, 1990.

Brunner, Emil. *Sowing and Reaping: The Parables of Jesus*, Trans. Thomas Wieser. Richmond: John Knox Press, 1946.

Buechner, Frederick. *Telling Secrets: A Memoir*. San Francisco: Harper, 1991.

Cartledge, Tony W. *Smyth & Helwys Commentary 1 & 2 Samuel*. Macon, Georgia: Smyth & Helwys, 2001.

Cooper-White, Pamela. *The Cry of Tamar: Violence against Women and the Church's Response*. Minneapolis: Fortress Press, 1995.

Domestic Violence Resource Center. "Domestic Violence Statistics." Accessed September 3, 2013. http://dvrc-or.org/domestic/violence/resources/C61/.

Ekman, Paul. *Why Kids Lie: How Parents Can Encourage Truthfulness*. New York: Charles Scribner's Sons, 1989.

Erikson, Erik. *Identity: Youth and Crisis*. New York: Norton, 1968.

Hogue, David. *Remembering the Future/Imagining the Past: Story, Ritual and the Human Brain*. Cleveland: Pilgrim Press, 2003

Huffstetter, Joel. *Boundless Love: The Parable of the Prodigal Son and Reconciliation*. Lanham, Maryland: University Press of America, 2008.

Hybels, Bill. *Transparency: Discovering the Rewards of Truth-Telling*. Grand Rapids: Zondervan, 1997.

Jenkins, Sara. *Past Present: Recording Life Stories of Older People*. Washington, D. C.: St. Alban's Parish, 1978.

Jeremias, Joachim. *Rediscovering the Parables*. New York: Charles Scribner's Sons, 1966.

Justes, Emma J. *Hearing beyond the Words: How to Become a Listening Pastor*. Nashville: Abingdon, 2006.

Komp, Diane M. *Anatomy of a Lie: The Truth about Lies and Why Good People Tell Them*. Grand Rapids: Zondervan, 1998.

Labecqz, Karen and Joseph D. Driskill. *Ethics and Spiritual Care: A Guide for Pastors, Chaplains and Spiritual Directors*. Nashville: Abingdon, 2000.

Lerner, Harriett G. *The Dance of Deception: Pretending and Truth Telling in Women's Lives*. New York: Harper Perennial, 1993.

Lewis, Vickie. *Side-by-Side: A Photographic History of American Women in War*. New York: Stewart, Tabori & Chang, 1999.

Malina, Bruce, and Richard L. Rohrbaugh. *Social-Science Commentary on the Synoptic Gospels*. Minneapolis: Fortress Press, 1992.

Mbiti, John. *African Religions and Philosophy*, Garden City: New York, 1970.

Morgan, Richard. *Remembering Your Story: Creating Your Own Spiritual Autobiography*. Nashville: Upper Room, 2002.

Nichols, Michael P. *The Lost Art of Listening*. New York: Guilford Press, 1995.

Penny, Louise. *A Trick of the Light*. New York: Minotaur, 2011.

Poling, Nancy Werking. *Victim to Survivor: Women Recovering from Clergy Sexual Abuse*. Cleveland: United Church Press, 1999.

Punt, Jeremy. "The Prodigal Son and the Blade Runner," *Journal of Theology for Southern Africa*, 128, 2007.

Rediger, G. Lloyd. *Clergy Killers: Guidance for Pastors and Congregations under Attack*. Louisville: Westminster John Knox, 1997.

Richardson, Ronald. *Creating a Healthier Church: Family Systems Theory, Leadership, and Congregational Life*. Minneapolis: Fortress Press, 1996.

Rutherford, Tom. "Reunited," *Guideposts*. [New York]: Guideposts Associates, January 2000.

Schacter, Daniel. *The Seven Sins of Memory: How the Mind Forgets and Remembers*. New York: Houghton Mifflin, 2001.

Scott, Bernard Brandon. *Hear Then the Parable: A Commentary on the Parables of Jesus*. Minneapolis: Fortress Press, 1989.

Smith, Alexander McCall. *The Ladies No. 1 Detective Agency*. New York: Anchor Books, 2002.

Smith, Harold Ivan. *A Long Shadowed Grief: Suicide and Its Aftermath.* Cambridge, Massachusetts: Cowley Publications, 2006.

Tournier, Paul. *Secrets.* Atlanta: John Knox Press, 1977.

Volf, Miroslav. *The End of Memory: Remembering Rightly in a Violent World.* Grand Rapids: Eerdmans, 2006.

Warren, Frank. *A Lifetime of Secrets.* New York: Harper/Collins, 2009.

———. *PostSecret: Confessions on Life Death, and God.* New York: Harper/Collins, 2009.

CPSIA information can be obtained at www.ICGtesting.com
Printed in the USA
LVOW11s1205250314

378795LV00005B/12/P